D1610862

RUNNING COMMENTARY

Dedicated to Nan Hardy – my
first coach and timekeeper

RUNNING COMMENTARY
An Autobiography

Dave Moorcroft
& Cliff Temple

Stanley Paul
London Melbourne Sydney Auckland Johannesburg

Stanley Paul & Co. Ltd
An imprint of the Hutchinson Publishing Group
17–21 Conway Street, London W 1 P 6J D

Hutchinson Publishing Group (Australia) Pty Ltd
PO Box 496, 16–22 Church Street, Hawthorne,
Melbourne, Victoria 3122

Hutchinson Group (N Z) Ltd
32–34 View Road, P O Box 40–086, Glenfield,
Auckland 10

Hutchinson Group (S A) Pty Ltd
PO Box 337, Bergvlei 2012, South Africa

First published 1984
© Dave Moorcroft and Cliff Temple 1984

Set in Linotron Baskerville by
Wyvern Typesetting Limited, Bristol

Printed and bound in Great Britain by
Anchor Brendon Ltd, Tiptree, Essex

British Library Cataloguing in Publication Data
Moorcroft, David
Running commentary.
1. Moorcroft, David   2. Runners (Sports)
– Great Britain – Biography
I. Title   II. Temple, Cliff
796.4'26'0924   GV1061.15.M6

ISBN 0 09 155200 1

Contents

Acknowledgements

I would like to acknowledge with gratitude the encourage-
ment and support I've received over the years from the
following people, without whom, as they say. . . Val and
Steve Baker (my sister and brother-in-law); John and
Hazel Ward (Linda's parents); Pauline Martyn; Jim and
Liz Eveleigh; Bet and Ron Morgan; John Camkin;
Andy Norman; the chairman, committee and staff of the
Coventry and Warwickshire Awards Trust; and all my
family and friends who have helped me through good
times and bad.

PHOTOGRAPHIC ACKNOWLEDGEMENTS

The author and publisher would like to thank Mark
Shearman for providing the bulk of the photographs in
this book. Other photographs were provided by the
Coventry Evening Telegraph, George Herringshaw, Bob Sly
and D. Straughan.

Introduction

At different times in my career, my running has achieved all shades of good and bad. But through it all I have been a happy runner in a sport which, through accident or design, has become such an important part of my life, and of those nearest to me.

Although it has been my performances which provide the accumulation of statistics, it is the story behind those results which really tells the tale. Even this book cannot do justice to the very many people who have been a part of the 'team' throughout the years. To each and every one of them, those who are named in the book and those who are not, I say a heartfelt 'Thanks'.

Fate has played its part. If I had passed my 11-plus, if I had passed my O-Levels first time, if I had . . .

But I did not. And this is the story of what happened next.

1

Midnight in Oslo

The reflection of the moon shone vividly like a bright, piercing light in the glass-smooth lake, and in the undergrowth beside me there was a sudden rustling as a nocturnal creature discovered to its surprise a human being sitting alone on a rock overlooking the water so late at night.

I scarcely noticed its arrival or departure, as my mind was still far away from this tranquil Norwegian setting. I leaned back on both elbows, and stretched out my legs. They felt light, almost restless, with not a trace of fatigue. Yet several hours earlier they had carried me twelve and a half times around an Oslo running track faster than anyone had run before. Anywhere. Ever.

It was hard to grasp. What was a world record holder supposed to feel? It was so unexpected that I had never even considered it, and only now had I managed to break away from the distractions which had followed me since I crossed the line in Bislett Stadium. Everyone meant well; they wanted to know how I had done it, how I had taken 6 seconds off the world 5000-metre record, running on my own. Yet how could I tell them when I did not even know myself?

I knew that around the world at this very moment sports editors would be looking at news agency reports coming in on their teleprinters and exclaiming, 'Dave Moorcroft? Broke the world 5000 record?'

I thought of home in Coventry and of Linda, my wife, who would be answering the telephone all evening to people ringing to see if she had heard. And I thought of our little boy, Paul, who had been fast asleep in his cot through it all, dreaming of sweets and teddy bears, and blissfully unaware that Daddy had done anything unusual. All he would know tomorrow was that Daddy was not there at breakfast to pick up his spoon.

I had needed to get away when the car brought me back to the hotel from the track. Inside I could already see people milling around the reception area, and I knew they would ask me, 'How did you do it?' I needed some answer. So I had turned away and instead walked through the semidarkness of this Norwegian midsummer night to the deserted lakeside.

My mind went back in time, past my recent training, and across eighteen years to when I was a small, skinny eleven-year-old, running round the local track in big shorts. It was an odd distance round, and a rough surface, but I lost count of the number of times I won Olympic gold medals or set world records there when I was eleven, before my dad took me home for tea.

How appropriate it was that he had actually been at that track himself tonight, timing other youngsters with heady dreams in a local meeting, when one of his son's boyish fantasies became reality.

All those days, all those years, of running through wind and rain, snow and ice, along seashores and up steep hillsides, had led to this. Breaking a world record was what I always dreamed about, and yet when it came it had taken me by surprise.

So often I had thought it impossible. In 1970 it would have been so easy to have given up. Later, at college, when I was so tired, and more recently, when my calves gave me so much pain that I could hardly stand up the day after a race, the temptation to say 'No more' was enormous. But I had kept going.

Athletics is not only about records, though. It is about winning races, or at least getting the best out of yourself. As I surveyed the peaceful setting, I had to face reality. By tomorrow night I could just as easily be an ex-world record holder if someone ran a split second faster. But

12

gold medals are different. They are what really matter. There were two I wanted to win in the next couple of months, and I knew that I must stop thinking that I was already at the peak of the mountain.

I stood up and started walking back through the forest paths towards the hotel. I had come to terms with what I had done: I was the world 5000-metre record holder, although the 1982 season had barely started.

Yet I had an uneasy feeling at the back of my mind that life was never going to be quite the same again.

2

Off and Running

When I think of that euphoric night in Oslo, I cannot help
drifting back in time to the day I felt my career had ended.
For I had finished last in a cross-country race, having hurt
my foot on the way round, and that day I really thought
the earth had crumbled beneath me. I was shattered.
Desolate. Inconsolable. And twelve.

I had been a member of the famous Coventry Godiva
Harriers for a year, and after my disaster in what had been
the Coventry Schools trial race, I thought I would go
along to watch a Birmingham League cross-country event
in the afternoon, before the letter I expected next Monday
arrived on the doormat, kicking me out of the club.

As I stood watching the Godiva seniors in action, with
internationals Dick and Juan Taylor controlling the race
and moving so effortlessly through the field, an official
from Godiva, Harry Lapworth, came up to me. He was
the club chairman, the driving force, and the Wisest Man
in Athletics so far as I was concerned. I felt sure he had
been appointed to be the club's hit man and was ready to
tip me the Black Spot.

Instead, he put his arm round me and said, 'Look, son,
I know you're unhappy with your run this morning, but
you've got to learn very quickly how to lose. This is the
first time you've come last, but it'll happen again. It
happens to every runner some time. And, after all, there
are many worse things in life than simply finishing last in
a race.'

I think my father must have asked him to have a word
with me, but it had exactly the right effect and helped me

to get things in perspective. Many years later, when a stomach bug left me weak and unable to get through the semifinals of the 1980 Olympics, I sat with Linda for ages afterwards talking about it. By then I was wholly committed to trying to win gold. But, after the initial disappointment, you simply have to get yourself back into the world again and go on living.

Whether it is a dispiriting run in a local schools race, or an Olympic Games for which you have devoted years of your life to training, you can never turn the clock back. Regardless of what some people say, it is, after all, only a sport.

I am sure that many people must have thought my own father, Bob, took it all too seriously when he used to come and watch my every sporting event from junior school onwards. He would always ensure that I had the right kit, and would often look white as a sheet himself before I ran a race. He never pushed me too hard, like some ambitious parents do, and he always knew exactly what to say if I did not run well, which was more often than not.

I was about nine or ten, and on a family holiday in Swanage, when he first noticed I had some running ability. He challenged me to a race round a cricket field, and although he was never a star, he kept himself quite fit, and was disconcerted to find I could outsprint him at the end of our 'race'.

But long before that, from when I was only three, I would sneak onto the old cinder track at the Butts Stadium at Earlsdon, in Coventry, and run round, or long jump, mimicking Olympic athletes like Basil Heatley and Brian Kilby, whom I must have seen training there, although I did not know who they were at the time. The stadium, which was long the home of Coventry Godiva Harriers, is little more than a rickety sit-here-at-your-own-risk stand with a non-standard 367-yard track round a soccer pitch.

Despite its primitive changing accommodation and dilapidated appearance, it nevertheless had a real sense of history about it, and to me, then, it was the finest stadium in the world. Only in 1984 did the club finally move to its new headquarters at the all-weather track at Warwick University. In recent years that track has been a pinnacle of my father's own enthusiasm, as a member of the fund-raising committee which put £120,000 towards its construction.

It is a far cry from that Sunday morning in 1964 when he first took me along to the Butts to join the club. He had always been interested in sport himself, although he worked for Massey-Ferguson as a draughtsman and is today a product planning manager with the same company.

My mother, Millie, was perhaps a typical athletics 'mum' in that she kept my kit clean, but did not particularly enjoy coming to watch me run because she felt, with maternal protectiveness, that it was simply not fair that bigger boys should be allowed to run against me. I do not think she really appreciated then that some boys mature more quickly than others, but she would occasionally shout out, 'Come *on*, David!' during a race as though she was mystified as to why I was not running any faster. On at least one occasion I am afraid I returned a comment which succinctly explained that I was feeling fairly tired.

Mum hails from Manchester, and met Dad on a train. He was in the Navy at the time, but was born and bred in Coventry, as I was. They married in 1946, and moved soon afterwards into the same semidetached house on Kenpas Highway in which they live today, and where I grew up.

So Coventry has always been my home, a city which developed and prospered in the fifties and sixties through the growth of the car industry. Today its population remains steady at around 300,000, although sadly there is a fairly high level of unemployment, which brings its own problems.

To most outsiders Coventry is always associated with Lady Godiva. She really existed, in the eleventh century, and was the wife of Leofric, Earl of Mercia and Lord of

Coventry. She was a devoutly religious and caring lady, and when her husband imposed new taxes on the people of Coventry, she begged him to reduce them. He agreed, but only on the condition, so the legend goes, that she would ride naked on a white horse through the market place.

So she did, with her long hair doubtless strategically arranged, and in turn, true to his word, Leofric reduced the taxes. (Funny how everyone remembers that she rode naked through the city, but no one remembers *why*. I wonder if the Inland Revenue could be similarly bribed today?)

The name Godiva is still very much alive in Coventry. The name Leofric lives on too, as one of the poshest hotels in the city bears that title. However, I have not seen too many naked girls on white horses in the city centre.

A great deal of the centre is new, following its destruction on the night of 14 November 1940. When the German Luftwaffe realized that it was not making sufficient impact by bombing such a sprawling city as London, it was ordered by Goering to switch its raids to provincial cities. Coventry was the first one to be attacked, and that night over 400 civilians died.

The shell of the destroyed Coventry Cathedral still stands today alongside the new one which was designed by Basil (later Sir Basil) Spence, and one of my earliest memories is of seeing the Queen come to Coventry in May 1962 for the consecration of the new cathedral. I was nine years old at the time, and in the Cubs.

Until I was eight I attended Styvchele Junior School, and then the junior school of King Henry VIII Grammar School, to which my parents hoped I would progress later. But I failed my 11-plus exam and was moved instead to Woodlands Comprehensive School, where the former pupils included Bill Adcocks, one of my heroes at that time as he was one of Britain's top road runners.

At school I could run quite fast, particularly when we played rugby. I was so scared of being tackled that the adrenaline alone would have powered me to Olympic

sprint victories up and down those muddy pitches. I
played rugby and soccer regularly, but I was never very
good. I remember reading something by Fred Ayer in
which he said that he was a two-footed player – equally
bad with either foot. Well, that went for me too. But
whenever it was too wet to play we would be sent off on a
cross-country run while the teachers nipped into the staff
room for a quick fag and a cup of coffee. I really enjoyed
running.

Even at eleven I had started to keep a training diary.
The enthusiasm rose and fell, I must admit, and looking
back to the little black 1965 diary now I see that
eventually my father took it over and finished it off. In the
early months, though, there are some neat entries in
schoolboy writing, usually telling a tale of woe even then.

Saturday, 20 February: Went to see Warwickshire Schools
championships at Bramcote. Woodlands [my school] did not
send a team.
Sunday, 21 February: Ran from Butts to Memorial Park and
ran 2½ laps, fell and cut finger, and had to return to Butts.
Wednesday, 24 February: Running from home up and down
Kenpas Highway hill. Found to be too much and stiffened up
next day.
Thursday, 25 February: Had long walk to try and remove
stiffness.
Friday, 26 February: Ran in Woodlands School inter-house
championship under-13. Came 2nd to Eales, about 8 seconds
away. Winner's time 9 min 1.8 sec.

On such occasions I invariably finished second to this
youngster Paul Eales, who was an inseparable com-
panion. We still occasionally find ourselves lining up
together for races today, nearly twenty years later, but
then we were constantly racing. We were the same height,
about the same level in school work, and neither of us was
brilliant academically.

We had even been born in the same ward at Gulson
Road Hospital, and almost on the same day too. My date

of birth was 10 April 1953, and Paul's 11 April 1953, so our mothers got to know each other before either of us was born.

As a runner Paul was better than I was in schools competitions. When we ran our junior district cross-country trials, over a distance of what seemed like forty miles but was probably nearer one and a half, I was twentieth and Paul was third or fourth. The first twenty were being sent to the Coventry Area trial, and this time, in a bigger race, Paul was second and, even more illogically, I was sixth.

In those early cross-country days I had a pair of special cross-country shoes. I think they were called Greengages and they looked like great big black hockey boots. They were made of canvas with rubber-studded soles – they were probably the forerunner of waffle-soled shoes – but appeared to be filled with lead and seemed to weigh about three tons each; four when wet. With my skinny arms and legs, plus these shoes and a pair of large gloves, on a muddy day I could have been mistaken for Mickey Mouse. Today I do not think I would feel all that comfortable racing nine miles in the English Cross-Country Championships in them, but at that time I thought they were fantastic.

In my third year at Woodlands School, when I was thirteen, I managed to make the Warwickshire county team for the 1966 English Schools cross-country championships, held that year in Derby. It was the biggest occasion to which I had ever been, and I was the youngest of the team. Although not frequently highlighted in the newspapers, the English Schools championships are always a memorable experience for the youngsters from all over the country, many of whom are away from home and their families for the first time. Although we did not have a long journey, it was still something of an adventure, as I had to go on my own on the team bus, whereas previously my father had always taken me everywhere.

But it was a marvellous learning experience too, and no

one was prouder than I was to wear the yellow vest and black tracksuit of my county. In the race itself, won by another Warwickshire boy, Martin Jones, I worked my way through to eighty-sixth place after being left at the start. I was only 300th after 150 yards, having naively thought that you were supposed to wait for the command 'Go!' I still found myself in the winning team, even though I had not finished high enough to be a scorer. The non-scorers were given winners' badges too, so I was very pleased when I got home.

Throughout my school career I was in the Warwickshire cross-country team and (although I am not claiming it was my doing) we always won. The other side of the coin, though, was that living in such a strong running county with athletes like Ray Smedley and Vince Rollason around, I was never able to earn selection for the English Schools track and field championships in the summer, which is even more of an exciting occasion.

But if that was, in the short term, a disappointment, I hope it will also serve as a reminder to young athletes today that failing to make their county team is not the end of the road, any more than finishing last in that Coventry Schools cross-country race had been for me. Some athletes who win English Schools titles are destined never to achieve anything higher. In fact, now I am almost proud of the fact that I did not reach the English Schools summer championships.

Reg Payne, my coach at that time, passed me and the rest of our group at Godiva on to Mick Crossfield, a physiotherapist by profession, and a former marathon exponent who had run 2 hours 25 minutes for the distance in 1963. I will never forget his first words to me. He said, 'Hello, I'm Mick Crossfield, but most people call me bastard!' He was certainly a stickler for hard training, but he was really dedicated to the junior section and used to take us to races all over the country.

We trained three times a week, which was probably quite sufficient for lads of our age, but eventually Mick realized that as a coach he had taken us about as far as he could, and in 1969 he asked for some guidance from John Anderson. At the time we youngsters did not understand much about coaching, or why we needed additional coaching advice at all. After all, we trained hard and we were doing well. But in retrospect it was a very courageous decision by Mick, because some coaches hold on to athletes for too long after they have exhausted their own limits of knowledge.

John Anderson, a mad, fiery Scot, was at that time Scottish national coach and living in Hamilton, but he coached Coventry Godiva Harriers' most successful lady athlete, Sheila Taylor (later Sheila Carey), who had finished fourth in the 1968 Olympic 800-metre final. John agreed to help and although at first I did not deal directly with him, leaving Mick and my father to keep in touch with him, it was the beginning of a very fruitful relationship which continues to this day. It was to provide a turning point, too, not only in my running career, but also in my whole life.

I officially began training under John's directions on 15 May 1969, and his first week's training programme for me as a sixteen-year-old was:

Sunday: (a.m.) $\frac{1}{2}$ hour steady run
        (p.m.) 4 × 660 yards
Monday: 1 hour fartlek
Tuesday: 20 slow/fast 220s
Wednesday: 1 hour fartlek
Thursday: 4 × 660 yards in 100 seconds with 4 minutes' recovery
Friday: Rest
Saturday: Race, or (a.m.) $\frac{1}{2}$ hour steady run
        (p.m.) 4 × 660 yards

My life until then had been unspectacular in terms of achievement. At school I had not placed too much importance on academic work. I saw school simply as a place to get through with the minimum of hassle. If you did as little as possible, without harming anyone or

21

getting into trouble, then that was success. One of the disadvantages (or, as I saw it then, advantages) of a school as big as Woodlands Comprehensive was that it was very easy to fade into the crowd, to become anonymous. If you did just enough work not to cause the teachers any problems, they would leave you alone.

I thought of myself as average, and did not have a great deal of confidence in my academic ability. Perhaps that was why I failed all of my GCE O-Levels. I took seven, and in each of them was given a Grade 7, whereas Grade 6 was the pass mark. This meant there were two options open to me: either to leave school and get an apprentice-ship, or to try to pass the O-Levels again at college. The motor trade around Coventry was buoyant at that time and most of the school teachers thought I should go for the apprenticeship. I was at a crossroads, even if I did not fully appreciate it then. What I really needed was time and space to think things over, away from home, Coventry, family, everything.

During the summer of 1970 the Commonwealth Games were being held in Edinburgh and so, at seventeen, I took a slight step into the outside world by going up to Scotland with Robin Godfrey, a mate from Coventry, to watch them. It was my first time away from home without the family and was a valuable experience. Digs were arranged for us and we ate cheap food whenever we could, saving money here and there. We had a great time.

I also got the chance to get to know John Anderson properly for the first time. Although he was now no longer Scottish national coach, having taken up an appointment as director of Physical Education at Heriot-Watt University in Edinburgh, he was still very involved with coaching some of the athletes taking part in the Games. Yet he found time to talk to me about my own running, and I spent a week after the Games with him which was most enlightening.

The euphoria of seeing the Games and the successes of great athletes like Kip Keino and Ron Hill was inspiring, especially when the Meadowbank Stadium shook with the noise of Scottish successes as Lachie Stewart won the 10,000-metre and Ian Stewart the 5000-metre gold medals. At that time I never dreamed of one day winning Commonwealth Games titles myself.

But I was hoping that a Coventry athlete would win gold in the women's 800-metre final in Edinburgh, for Sheila Carey was in spectacular form. I trained with her both in Coventry and while I was in Scotland, and it was partly through her that I had met John. She had an outstanding chance of winning, but in the final, after the eight-girl field had run the first bend in lanes then merged on the inside in the back straight, the crowd gasped as one of the runners tripped and went crashing heavily to the ground. For a brief moment none of us could see who it was. Then our worst fears were confirmed. The girl slowly getting to her feet to begin a hopeless chase after the disappearing field was Sheila.

To see her so bitterly upset after the race, in which she could do no more than finish eighth after lining up with such strong hopes of gold, was a sobering experience, and another lesson for the future. Some people have said that she still might not have beaten Rosemary Stirling, who delighted the home crowd by winning another gold medal for Scotland, but I believed she would have done, judging by her training sessions. But the real frustration for Sheila came in not being able to test herself properly through such a cruel misfortune. It was disappointing that she had to lose in that way.

For me, it was a week of indelible memories, witnessing a major games for the first time, sharing with Sheila and John in their disappointment and, above all, being subjected to long doses of John's irrepressible character for two weeks.

Until that time, I did not really have great confidence in any walk of life. In some ways, perhaps, I still do not. But it was in 1970 that I began to realize that I would not be content always to gravitate towards the average. I had relied on a lot of people up to that point, and had done relatively little for myself. But that time in Edinburgh gave me a heady taste of independence, a new future, fired by John's ceaseless enthusiasm.

Although sometimes now I appear to my family and friends to be a little removed or detached, it is simply my way of doing things on my own. Underneath, I have a dogged, even stubborn, determination, even if I seem outwardly shy and reserved. But that summer of 1970 I look upon now as a turning point. I had to conquer my own insecurity and a reluctance to become someone different. Sometimes I have to continue that fight today. But from that time I began to put together the bones of being an independent person.

I had been heading for mediocrity. After all, the structure of society depends on people being average in vast numbers. It is only the odd nutcase who wants to do something special who causes trouble. But the time in Scotland was crucial. Being away from the family for the first time, making mistakes, getting drunk and having a hangover, was like attending the School of Life for someone who had been relatively sheltered during his childhood.

From Scotland I went with John down to the AAA Junior Championships at Kirkby in Liverpool, and managed to reach the final of the 1500 metres, running a personal best of 3:57.8 in the heats and another best of 3:55.7 for sixth place in the final. As a pointer to my athletics career, it was a huge step forward, and I felt that perhaps my new approach to life was already beginning to work.

Back home in Coventry I still had to decide on my professional future. Should I take up the apprenticeship in the car industry, or try to improve my academic status? My seven GCE failures had all been narrow ones, after all. In my new frame of mind it did not need a great deal of chewing over. Along with a considerable number of other GCE failures, I enrolled at Tile Hill College of Further Education, determined to do better this time.

In my own mind, though, I was already happier. John had convinced me that it was worth taking my running career seriously, and that I should make the most of myself as an all-round person. I was phoning him virtually every night for more of his direct brand of motivation. Perhaps also, although I did not admit it at the time even to myself, for some reassurance that I was doing the right thing. Yet I knew I was. After the initial failures, I felt that things could only improve from now on. I was off and running.

3

Arrival – and Departure

Most of the other pupils at Tile Hill College were either mature students or else youngsters retaking their O-Levels, like me. But the two years I spent there turned out to be most eventful, not least because I met my future wife there.

I had already made up my mind to work hard with my newly developed philosophy, and to make the most of my second chance. But that did not stop me going to some of the many parties which were a regular feature of college after-hours activity, and I could not help noticing a particular brunette, whose name was Linda Ward.

She had come to the college from secondary modern school because she could not take the O- and A-Levels she wanted there, and to do a secretarial course. So she was not a failure like me.

For the first few months we did not get to know each other well. She used to turn up at the same parties as I went to, but with a bloke in tow, so, full of self-confidence, I did not go anywhere near her. Then one night (at a rough guess I would say it was 22 January 1971) she came to a party alone. So I switched on my debonair chatting-up approach, complimenting her on her dress and asking if she had made it herself. I cannot remember now whether she had or not, but at the time I managed to affect a keen interest in dressmaking for an hour or two.

Towards the end of the evening she asked me how I was getting home (or perhaps it was *when* was I going home?). I told her I had run to the party, then nearly bit off my tongue because I could imagine her replying, 'So that's the funny smell.' Instead, she told me that her father was coming to collect her, and that she was sure he would give me a lift.

I said 'No, no, I've got to run back too. I need the mileage.'

Then it occurred to me that I might not see her again. So I went by car, and damned the mileage.

For the first year at the college, as Linda and I started to go steady, Linda studied hard and added a couple of O-Levels to the six she already had, and an A-Level. I worked much harder than I had done at school. But I found time to take part in basketball and soccer, and performed as Chief Fairy in a college play. I even managed to pass four O-Levels too.

Linda and I decided to take the same courses the following year. We both wanted to go to teacher training college, so we signed on for English and economics at A-Level, with a couple of subsidiary O-Level subjects. I took maths, for about the fifteenth time, and something else which I cannot remember. Probably dressmaking. As it turned out, we both passed our A-Level exams thanks particularly to a very helpful lady lecturer named Jo De Lange.

I also became quite fit during my first year. My daily routine was to run from home to college, stopping off on the way at my Aunt Edie's house. She lived about a quarter of a mile from the college and when I had finished my run she would feed me up with a cooked breakfast every morning. This pleasant routine ended when I passed my driving test at seventeen – the first exam in my life I had actually passed! After that I used to collect Linda in my Mum's car.

At that time I had been running well enough to be selected as twelfth man for Coventry Godiva Harriers in the AAA national twelve-stage road relay championship at Sutton Coldfield and, petrified by the responsibility, ran what turned out to be the fastest lap on the shorter of the two courses which are used during the race.

From that performance I was able to run as a guest in a

1500-metre race in the match between the Midland Counties and British Universities at Birmingham, and then in an invitation 1500 metres at the Inter-Counties Championships, where I finished second to Commonwealth Games 5000-metre silver medallist Ian McCafferty in 3:48.5. From that, I was selected for the AAA team to meet Loughborough Colleges in a traditional and exciting fixture at Loughborough itself.

After my race that evening, in which I finished second to John Kirkbride though sharing the winning time of 3:46.1, I was chatting to one of the Loughborough lecturers, a Greek named Basil Stamatakis. He had for many years been the driving force behind Loughborough's fine athletics reputation, and was then deputy head of Physical Education. He asked me what I wanted to do academically.

'I'd like to teach,' I told him.

'Well, have you considered coming to Loughborough?' he asked.

'I'd love to,' I said, 'but don't you have to be academically brilliant for that?'

'You're doing two A-Levels, aren't you?' he replied. 'Why don't you give it a go?'

So I applied, although it would never otherwise have occurred to me, and I thought there would be little chance of my being accepted at such an illustrious place.

As a result of that race at Loughborough, which was equivalent to about 4 minutes 4 seconds for the mile, I was invited to run in the 1971 Emsley Carr Mile, the traditional invitation event which that year was being held in Edinburgh. One newspaper even asked 'Will Moorcroft become the first British 18-year-old to break four minutes for the mile?', a somewhat rash question.

I was scared out of my mind at the prospect, and that week I was also taking part in another college play. This time I was a Yorkshire mill owner, with an accent which was not only different on each of the four nights we performed, but actually tended to change during the course of each performance. I was absolutely terrible, but quite enjoyed the experience, and was in two minds as to whether to go to Edinburgh and so miss the last night celebrations after the play, as well as the final performance. But the college assured me they had managed to find someone who was almost as bad an actor as I was to stand in, so that was all right.

When I got to Edinburgh, I remember Brendan Foster pulling my leg and saying to me, 'So you're the young bloke who's going to break four minutes tomorrow?' And I was babbling away, saying, 'No, no, no, it wasn't me who said that. The paper said it, not me. I didn't say it.' It took me a while to realize he was winding me up.

It was a time when British distance running was starting to pick up again, through the likes of Brendan, Ian Stewart, my own club-mate Dick Taylor, and particularly the flamboyant Dave Bedford.

My confidence was somewhat strengthened on the flight up to Edinburgh. I was sitting next to one of the leading British runners of that time, an experienced major games medallist and UK record breaker. As we approached the airport to land, a gust of wind caught the plane and the pilot suddenly had to take it up again to make a second attempt at a landing approach. The runner next to me was petrified, and kept shouting, 'We're going to crash, we're going to crash!' As he had flown all over the world, and I had barely travelled at all, yet knew we were not going to crash, my view of his exalted image changed somewhat. I have my own insecurities, but like most people I usually try to disguise them.

The wind at Meadowbank, not for the first or last time, affected all performances in the meeting, the British International Games, and in the Emsley Carr Mile no one broke 4 minutes. Peter Stewart won in 4:00.4, and I was ninth in 4:07.5. It was experience, anyway.

Our second year at college was a great deal of fun and Linda and I enjoyed attending classes together. I used to pick her up by car each morning, and as she was seldom ready, we usually ended up arriving at the last moment. Then she would sneak into the class, leaving me to park the car and endure the daily reprimand, 'Moorcroft, you're always late.'

If I were to nominate the most important years of my life, I would choose the time I spent at Tile Hill. All through school I had been sheltered by the institution and had managed to manipulate things so that I did the minimum amount of work. Once I had failed my O-Levels, I realized how important it was to study, and I think that carried over into my running and into my life generally.

Both Linda and I became more adult in those two years. We went to parties and lunchtime pub get-togethers, mixing as mini-adults and learning a lot about life. The college was new, the lecturers were young, and it was a stimulating atmosphere.

Before we finished at Tile Hill, Linda and I decided that if we managed to get into teacher training college, we would go to separate places as we had already spent so much time together at Tile Hill. I was due to go to Loughborough for an interview, so Linda applied to a college in Leicester, which was not too far away.

My interview included a physical aptitude test, which all Loughborough students are asked to take, and for me was a little bit like asking a middle-distance runner to perform in 'TV Superstars'. I approached my test with trepidation. I was all right at ball games, like basketball, but when the dreaded moment came to perform a handstand, I could not do it. 'Why don't you try one against the wall?' suggested the examiner sympathetically as I fell in a distorted crumpled heap on the floor. The wall was much better. At least it gave me something solid to crumple and distort against.

Then they brought out a gymnasium box, which looked about 20 feet high, and a springboard. I was sweating buckets by now; what was I going to do? All the other would-be students were bounding down, flying gracefully through the air and performing immaculate handsprings and somersaults. When my turn came, I ran towards the box and took off, hoping that something would happen. I thought that maybe you just leaped into the air and instinctively performed a somersault. But, as I discovered, you do not. Instead, you land heavily on top of the box and then slide, like a sack of potatoes, off the other side so that everyone comes and stands anxiously round you while you lie there groaning.

How I was ever accepted for Loughborough after that I will never know. I certainly was not the greatest gymnast ever to pass through their hallowed grounds. Perhaps it was my sheer foolhardiness. Or perhaps they saw in me good material for any future kamikaze raids on their great rivals, Borough Road College (now the West London Institute).

The summer of 1972 was not exceptional so far as my running was concerned. Early in the season I had run a personal best mile – 4:03.3 – finishing fourth in the Ceylon Tea Meeting at Crystal Palace, but in June on the same track I tailed off in tenth place in the Emsley Carr Mile. Peter Stewart won in a UK record of 3:55.3, and led four others below 4 minutes, but I ran 4:18.5. 'Terrible run. Very tense,' I wrote in my training diary.

Several weeks later I ran the 1500 metres for Britain in a junior international match against Sweden in Härnosand, finishing fourth of six in 3:56.4; Barry Smith won in 3:54.5. The only saving grace that summer was a personal best 1500 metres of 3:45.7 in the heats of the AAA Championships in mid-July. But it was not enough to reach the final.

Sheila Carey had been running well earlier in the summer and although she had been hampered by illness, which meant that she only just scraped into the British Olympic team for Munich by winning an eleventh-hour selection race, both she and John had been working hard towards something much better in the Games themselves.

The 1972 Olympics were, of course, for ever marred by the murder of members of the Israeli team by Palestinian terrorists who broke into the Olympic village complex at night. But the athletics themselves were inspiring. Sheila was the only British girl to reach the final of the 1500

31

metres, setting U K records of 4:07.4 in her semifinal and 4:04.8 in the final, where she finished a fine fifth. She had improved by over 11 seconds during the Games, and her final time would have constituted a world record *before* the Games.

Brendan Foster also finished fifth in the men's 1500-metre final but it was his determined run in the semifinals which really inspired me. He pushed the pace along to try to blunt the fast finishers, was passed by a group at the bell, but fought back to get a place in the final in third position, equalling the U K record of 3:38.2 in the process.

Watching those events on television helped to invigorate me again following my own disappointing season. I felt a need to put down on paper my inner feelings at the time, and I still have the dog-eared piece of college file paper on which I wrote the following:

Today is Saturday, 9 September, during the Olympic Games, the day of Sheila Carey's final and the semifinals of the men's 1500-metres where Brendan Foster showed the guts and determination required of a champion, and became the only Briton to reach the final.

The past few days have been inspiring from the running point of view, and it has also been a time of realizing a few home truths. Right! Last season (1971) you improved from 3:55.7 to 3:46.1 and won the A A A junior 1500-metre championship. You showed no fear of anyone and remained quite consistent. This year (1972) has been very poor, inconsistent, with not enough confidence and determination. Although there was one reasonably high point, the A A A heats, a personal best of 3:45.7, most of the races were very poor.

The remedies are simple and hard. Simple to say, yet hard to do, but the result will be worth it if. . . ? There is no doubt in my mind, I know you can do it. It's in your hands. You have the best coach in the world, enthusiasm from everyone around (parents, Linda, relatives, friends) and the ability. The other factors need strengthening.

The end product must be Dave Moorcroft, well trained, strong, utterly determined to win, convinced of your ability, relaxed yet rock hard, modest yet convinced.

The changes that need to be made are: harder, consistent training. I think up to now you have been going too much through the motions, there is no easy way out. Weight training must be continued and improved, the arms are very important, and at the end of the race strength is imperative.

The other things are better tactical appreciation, more determination providing consistency, become harder and *win*. It's man against man and you must be sure you are the best man bar none. It's the only way. The one who wins is the best prepared not only physically, but mentally. It is up to you. You must dig deeper and deeper all the time. Fear no one, respect everyone and be the first to the tape. Remember no one shall pass you when you break for the line. Good luck, mate, you can and will do it. The first step to the top starts this winter at Loughborough, a hard winter is required. You must fit all sessions in. It will be worth it.

On my arrival at Loughborough that autumn I was not quite sure what to expect. It has changed now, but at that time the colleges were basically divided into two sections: the PE students, who were known as 'jocks', and the creative design students, who were nicknamed 'chippies'. At that time Loughborough University (which later absorbed the colleges) was thought of as a group of academics on top of the hill.

Not surprisingly, the atmosphere tended to be dominated by the jocks, who were more prone to push the male macho image. Rugby was a keenly supported sport, and Steve Smith, later England's captain, who had just left, was still a legend, while Fran Cotton was there during my first year.

I quickly palled up with two other distance runners: Terry Colton from Worksop, whom I knew from past track skirmishes, and Dave Driver from Northampton. They were in the next rooms to me in the college's residential tower block. Terry had just come back from watching the Munich Olympics and was really inspired. Every morning he would be out for an early-morning training run, and the first two days I joined him. On the third, I stayed in bed. The trouble was that there was so much physical activity on the syllabus – three or four practical sessions each day – that trying to train for running after having swum, played rugby and clambered around the gymnasium was exceedingly difficult.

As a group we got on well together. My own section of around twenty students was nicknamed the PIGS because our official designation was P (for physical education), I for first year, and G (for Group G). We even had PIG tee-shirts made up with everyone's name on them. It took a little while to get used to the atmosphere at Loughborough, which was so different from that at Tile Hill. It was another stage of life, mixing with people from different backgrounds, different parts of the country and different sports, yet all studying PE together.

The only disappointing aspect was that Linda had not been accepted for college in Leicester, and instead had to go to Crewe College ninety miles away. She took an English, primary teaching and remedial studies course.

But, by an incredible coincidence, a student on my floor at Loughborough, Ian Smith, had a girlfriend at Crewe College too. So every Wednesday evening Ian used to travel up in his ramshackle old van with me as a passenger, returning early on Thursday in time for the first lecture. Another student, Paul Brocklebank, also gave me some lifts up to Crewe. After he left college I was to bump into him again teaching in the same school as me – in New Zealand!

The 1973 season began reasonably well, and although my sixteenth place in the National Junior Cross-Country Championships at Parliament Hill was four places lower than in 1972, our Loughborough Colleges team – Steve Galloway (twenty-seventh), Steve Carter (thirty-fifth), Terry Colton (thirty-eighth) and me – won the team title. Our score of 116 points was exactly the same as that of our deadly rivals, Borough Road College, and we won only on the position of our last scorer. But the exciting finish set off all sorts of controversy about whether specialist PE colleges should be allowed to compete against ordinary club teams in such events. Today they no longer can.

In April I ran the fastest short-stage leg in the AAA national twelve-stage road relay. Then in May I finished fourth in the Inter-Counties mile (4:07.7), and in June was second to Phil Banning over 1500 metres in the British International Games at Meadowbank in 3:42.9, a personal best.

That second place earned me my first British senior international vest for the match against East Germany in Leipzig shortly afterwards. The trip turned out to be a little less glamorous than the starry life of a globe-trotting international athlete about which I had long dreamed. On the journey out we got on the plane some three hours late, then had a long journey in a rickety bus in Germany, arriving in the dead of night at an apparently closed hotel, where there was no food or drink. It was a great experience to be in a team alongside an Olympic champion like Mary Peters, as well as Mike Bull and Dave Travis, and Sheila Carey from my own club, who helped me a great deal by explaining what was going on.

I spent most of the time with 800-metre runner Dave McMeekin from Scotland, whom I knew from the Great Britain junior team the previous year, and with whom I shared a room. One of the highlights of the weekend for the new internationals was the handing out of the official GB kit. My tracksuit trousers were too long, the top was too short, and the shorts were too big, but at least the shoelaces were a perfect fit. Strangely, I've never seen an official in an ill-fitting tracksuit, though.

The lowlight must have been the team meeting where all the newcomers were introduced, to some ribald heckling from some of the more boisterous members of the team, like shot putter Geoff Capes. My own race was fairly forgettable. I was teamed up with Phil Banning, and after a slow start we were both outkicked by the German

Klaus-Peter Justus (who the following year was destined to become European champion) in 3:44.7. Phil was second in 3:45, with me third in 3:45.5, ahead of a second German who was never heard of again. Afterwards the team coach in charge of the middle-distance events came up to me and said, Well done, and sorry he hadn't actually seen the race but . . .

As an introduction to international athletics, it had not been ecstatic, and worse was to follow. In the evening we went to the official reception where someone seemed to have forgotten to order any food, and I was so thirsty that I seized several glasses of wine. It was a mistake. Soon I felt the room spinning round, and eventually I was staggering so much that Dave McMeekin and his fellow Scot Frank Clement had to carry me back to the hotel and put me to bed. By 5 a.m. I was wide awake, feeling the desperate need for a cup of tea and some fresh air to clear my head. I got up, but there was no sign of life in the hotel, so, feeling unlikely to sleep if I went back to bed, I went out for a walk. Outside, in the streets of Leipzig, I was astonished to find hundreds of people, all on their way to work. It could have been a typical Monday morning anywhere, yet the buzz of activity so early in the morning amazed me.

I walked through the streets, feeling like a spy in a Frederick Forsyth novel, and found myself at Leipzig Station, where there were crowds of commuters pouring into the city. It could have been Victoria or Waterloo in the rush hour. On a wall a loudspeaker blared out announcements in a staccato tone which made them sound like orders from above.

Still gasping for a drink, I made my way to the buffet, where the system proved a little different from the typical British Rail establishment. The place was full of people having a standard breakfast on their way to work. Apparently you were supposed to have the breakfast before you took a drink. Consequently, my efforts at buying a drink were not entirely successful, especially as I proffered a large-denomination note which no one could change. In the end, I think the staff took pity on me and gave me a drink anyway. It was the foulest liquid I had ever tasted, and scarcely worth the effort, although I did appreciate their gesture. The experience was an eye-opener, but nevertheless I felt grateful at the thought that by the time these people would be making their way home from work that evening, I would be back in Coventry.

The East Germans take sport very seriously and, with some of the other British athletes, I had already had a chance to visit the famous Leipzig National Institute of Sport. Although Loughborough was pretty advanced among British colleges, it was quite a contrast to see the fantastic equipment they had in Leipzig and the earnestness of the students compared with some of the drunken jocks who went off the rails and fell apart at home!

During our first year at Loughborough we had to be able to perform all athletics events. I even got to the point where I could pole vault above my own height, which must rank as one of the greatest achievements of my athletics career. We were supposed to take all our studies very seriously, but it was difficult to sit indoors and study a film of world record breakers like Kjell Isakkson of Sweden and Bob Seagren of the USA vaulting superb heights in the Californian sunshine, then go out to a cold, blustery sports field with a freezing metal pole and try to do the same thing.

I almost won a pole-vault competition in the Midland League, when I cleared a couple of modest heights, then went off to run in the 5000 metres. By the time I came back someone else had fallen on the crossbar and broken it, and as no one could find another one, the event was abandoned.

Normally, though, it was like flogging a dead horse to try to get distance runners to perform field events well. We would study a film of former Commonwealth champion Howard Payne throwing the hammer, watching for the finer points of correct technique like hip placement, then

37

go out and do our best simply to avoid the hammer wire winding round our necks and throttling us.

When it came to the triple jump, we needed a relay team. I would start off doing my hop, step and jump from the take-off board, then Terry Colton would take over with his, and between us we could just about reach the sand pit. I actually got an A-minus for my triple jumping technique and by the time I left I could manage a cumulative jump approaching the women's world long-jump record. In long jumping we had to demonstrate the hitch kick, which is a series of running steps in mid-air after take-off and exceptionally difficult to perform when you are only jumping about 12 feet with a gale behind you.

When I had to do my 400-metre assessment, I came straight from a swimming session, and my cold muscles managed to get me round in about 52 seconds. I was quite pleased, but at Loughborough they never stop telling you about the times run by Olympic silver medallists Robbie Brightwell and John Cooper in the early sixties. Or about the day a talented youngster called Jon English ran 49:6 in a pair of flip-flops (though no one can remember *why*).

Then there was the steeplechase, which produced all sorts of styles, with some students hurdling straight over the water-jump barrier and into the icy depths, or the unfortunate soul who caught his trailing foot and plunged head first into the murky water. We all rushed up, expecting him to be dead at least, but he came out smiling and carried on running. That's what they like at Loughborough – hard men with broken necks!

When I ran a steeplechase, my technique was so bad that it took me longer to get over the barriers than to run between them. At the water jump I would stand with both feet on the hurdle, then leap across the water shouting 'Geronimo!' An unusual style, certainly, but it kept my shoes dry.

4

The Fiery Scot

During the years at college, one of the perennial problems was getting on the public telephone. Everyone wanted to use it, and I had to queue for hours sometimes to stick a few coins in the box in order to speak to Linda. It is hard to express your innermost emotions to the love of your life with a dozen impatient jocks standing behind you looking ostentatiously at their wristwatches. Sometimes I had to miss my call to Linda and instead phone John Anderson in Scotland to keep in touch over training.

George Gandy was in charge of athletics at Lough-borough by then, and he was extremely helpful in that he let the athletes there follow their own schedules if they wanted to, or join in with those he coached (who included Terry Colton), or a little of both. This was an ideal situation for me, as sometimes I was glad of company on training runs. My schedule was prepared by John, and it was a great help to me when he decided to leave Scotland in 1975 and move to Nuneaton, not far from Coventry, to take up a post there as Chief Leisure and Recreation Officer.

In the succeeding years I was to get to know John much better, but even today very few people actually understand this apparently raucous extrovert with a Glaswegian accent you could cut with a knife. And while I think I understand him better than most people, I do not think anyone will ever understand him fully. His unique obsession with athletics, with bringing out the best in people, and sometimes his sheer doggedness have admittedly not made him everybody's favourite person in

39

a sport where reputations and power are guarded as closely as in show business. I can imagine John as a barker for a travelling fair, or even as a highly successful roadside salesman.

There is not a trace of dishonesty in John, and in the past he has been badly hurt when he has discovered it in other people whom he has trusted. As a talker, he could persuade Eskimos to import five million tons of snow, but only if he really believed they needed it.

He was born in the tough Gorbals district of Glasgow, and there you had to fight to survive. If there was a choice between fighting or running, John would always stay and fight. But one of the best recent descriptions of him said that 'both his natural belligerence and his red hair have faded now'. I have never seen him hit anyone, although I have seen him apparently come close once or twice.

Through hard work as a boy he earned a place in a grammar school where he was fanatical about fitness. He was a good all-round games player, but tried every sport possible to become the *best* at something: soccer, bowls, athletics, tennis and even ice hockey. He was average to good, but fiercely tenacious, at everything. Later, he attended Jordanhill Training College, and played soccer (his first love) for Scottish Schoolboys and for Queen's Park in the Scottish Amateur League, before moving on to a career as a teacher.

It was at his first school in Glasgow that an elderly colleague first asked him to help coach a sprint relay team which was due to represent the school at a forthcoming sports day. Athletics as such was virtually unknown in that part of the city, but John's team was successful, and he soon became involved with Maryhill Athletic Club, first by simply taking some youngsters from his school along, then, as a PE teacher, by being asked to help with the coaching. He helped to build up the club, which later became Maryhill Ladies AC (and is now the City of Glasgow AC), in to one of the best in Britain in a very short time, through his own energy and vision, quickly

organizing parents to be assistant coaches and adminis-
trators.

In 1965 he moved into full-time coaching as the
peripatetic national coach for the Amateur Athletic
Association, and spent an exhausting eighteen months
travelling the length and breadth of the country in what
was probably a job of impossible requirements. In 1967 he
became Scottish national coach, a position he held for
three years, and it was at this time that I first met him.

To me, the epitome of a good coach is one who can drag
out of you performances of which you did not think you
were capable. He has certainly done that with me,
because whereas he always had the character to be a great
athlete, but not the physical ability, I had the ability, but
not the character. Yet he has done much more than that
for me. Probably few of his athletes have actually taken
advantage of John's approach to life in general to elevate
themselves as human beings, but I know I have.

Sometimes it can be difficult for a coach to instil a desire
to win in someone, even if he or she has the ability.
Perhaps in that respect I may be his biggest success,
because I was certainly not the most talented athlete he
ever coached.

At the time John took over my training in 1969 there
could have been, in similar circumstances, some conflict
with a father who had helped to look after his son's
training and development as an athlete from the start. But
my father was always very reasonable in this respect. He
could see the turning of the tide and the long-term
benefits. In any case, he was not one of those fathers who
puts pressure on a son or daughter if they perform below
par (and there are plenty of parents like that in sports far
removed from athletics). Instead, he was happy to
become the intermediary who wrote to and telephoned
John and in turn passed on John's instructions and
schedules to me in those early days. He would come to
training sessions and races, but never interfere. As time
passed, he could see that I was developing both as an
athlete and a person under John's influence.

With all his athletes, John makes it clear that he is the coach and the parent is the parent. He will not interfere in the parental role, but he does not expect a parent to interfere in the coach's role. And with us it certainly caused no problem.

Although he is not physically big, John has an intimidating presence. I remember on one occasion during the 1970 Commonwealth Games we were driving through Edinburgh with John's young nephew in the back when a car pulled sharply out in front of us. John sounded his horn vigorously. The driver turned and made, shall we say, a derisive gesture and John immediately saw red. He chased the car frenziedly through the back streets of the city, bouncing over the cobbled roads, until it finally stopped. As the driver got out of his car, John got out too, marched up to him – he was not a small man – and shoved him against the car. For a moment it looked like fisticuffs might follow, but the other man backed off and the incident ended peacefully. But John had been extremely annoyed at this man's reaction, especially with youngsters in the car.

On another occasion, a few years later, we were eating in a London restaurant with Linda, and Sheila and Peter Carey, when two big men at a nearby table began shouting and swearing. John went up to them and asked them politely if they would desist as there were ladies present and we all found their language embarrassing. They took no notice. So John went up to them again and said very quietly, 'Look, I think the best thing would be if you and I go outside and sort this out.' Their courage at that moment seemed to desert them, and we were able to finish our meal in peace.

John cannot tolerate an injustice. Usually when he gets into verbal scrapes it is over athletes who then leave him in the lurch. I have seen him have a protracted argument with a groundsman who wanted to take away a pole-vault pit on which an athlete was trying to train, only for the athlete concerned to back off and say he had finished training anyway.

42

Sadly, in other circumstances, John has sometimes been let down by athletes he has tried to help; he understandably gets very hurt when this happens. Maybe it is because he is not a cynic, for people who are habitually cynical rarely trust anyone else, so they are always expecting to be let down. But John trusts people, and in a highly individual sport like athletics, athletes themselves can be extremely selfish and introspective, and are very good at letting other people down.

Although he has mellowed a lot since I first knew him, he still cannot suffer fools easily, and he finds it difficult to stomach the perpetual power struggle among the officials who are fighting for prestige.

Our own relationship has gradually evolved, and he may have been slowly brainwashing me to the point where the opinions I now think are mine are probably really his. But a good coach does not smother the athlete, or try to make him coach-dependent. He makes him *in*dependent. When I went away to college at Loughborough in 1972, for instance, the independence John had encouraged in me certainly paid off, whereas I know a lot of other athletes who fell apart when they left home as they tried to come to terms with their academic work, their new-found freedom and social life, the mysteries of launderettes, the opening hours of McDonald's hamburger bars, and the need to maintain a high degree of self-discipline.

It has always surprised me that Sebastian Coe's relationship with his father has worked. He is such an extremely aggressive, competent competitor on the track, and yet apparently so dependent on Peter Coe. What Peter has obviously done is to create an independence on the track and that is, I believe, what John has done with me.

On the track I am a very committed athlete. It is not 'I want to win for Britain' or 'I want to win because I'm scared of John Anderson'. It is a very basic, animal-like, simplistic attitude. I just want to beat everybody else.

But I am not at all uncompromising in other situations.

Although at work I am a fairly demanding boss, I do believe in democracy, and am sometimes quite happy to go along with the majority opinion. Yet on the track I do not worry at all about how other people will feel if I beat them. A lot of athletes and coaches talk a great deal of nonsense about the need for a 'killer instinct'. Some athletes even go round spitting fire and growling at people. Yet I am sure they only do it to hide their insecurity. I do not bother to hide mine. It is there for all to see, as I try to tie up my spiked shoes with trembling fingers before a race.

Certainly I do not feel it betrays any disastrous weakness to admit the need for the support of a coach. Even after ten years of international athletics, as I approach, I hope, my third Olympics, I need John's guidance as much as ever, although obviously in a different way now. Perhaps what all athletes need is a guru to bring out the desire to be a winner, as much as someone simply to set a training schedule.

These days my thinking on race preparation is so closely allied to John's that if we were in different places and both independently wrote out a training programme to build up to a certain race, I can practically guarantee that both schedules would be the same. But where John is so valuable is in making me believe in myself. He made me believe I could run 13 minutes for 5000 metres, and he is rarely wrong in his predictions. He has great vision.

Unfortunately, and this is a point on which we agree to disagree, John's biggest problem is that he cannot say no when people ask him to help. And when he takes something on, he will not do it in half measures. Consequently, he has to devote every spare minute to coaching, and the more people he takes on, the less time he has for each of them. I am sure that it was this obsession which led at least in part to his divorce.

After his spell as director of PE at Heriot-Watt University, John came down to Nuneaton absolutely determined that he would only coach me, Dave Driver, and one or two others. But gradually, inevitably, his squad grew, for one of the problems of the successful coach is that athletes flock to him to the point where the very success he once achieved is in danger of being undermined by a subsequent dilution of attention.

To aggravate matters, John is not just a middle-distance specialist. It is typical of him that he coaches everything: sprinting, discus throwing, marathon running, hurdling and even the decathlon. That in turn stretches him logistically, even though he is very good technically and can put a tremendous fund of knowledge into operation for any event you care to name. But in 1979–80, for instance, his group was getting very large, and I was not receiving much personal attention. It did not bother me particularly but it bothered John, and he came to me one day and said he felt he had let me down by taking on so many people. 'I can understand it if you think I'm not giving you enough time,' he said. What he was really saying was that he would understand if I wanted to end our relationship. I assured him that it did not worry me, but that, yes, he did coach too many people. I knew, however, that it was not his fault. People kept asking, and he genuinely found it difficult to turn them away. Since then, though, things have been much better. But he still coaches a large number of athletes.

When John started coaching me, he always said that the idea was for me to become a good senior, not necessarily a good junior, although if that happened on the way it would be a bonus. His main belief is the importance of the acquisition of speed, and that is an ongoing process which involves both keeping what you already have and trying to gain more. I was never naturally fast, but he has largely succeeded in developing my ability to sprint quickly at the end of a race, for although I am still not too hot in a straight sprint, I can go quite fast when fatigued.

Yet sometimes there is a high price to pay for that, because although using year-round fast repetition 300-, 600- and 1000-metre runs, as in my training programme, is the way to become very good, you run the risk of injury because the strain is so great. But the alternative would be to perform less intensive track work in training, and also be a lesser runner.

Ideally, the ambitious athlete needs an ability to recover quickly and correctly in order to maintain the level of training which will bring improvement. In the early days I probably trained too hard and raced too often without paying sufficient attention to recovering fully in between, and the penalty for that is being paid now through my having more injuries later in my career.

My attempts in recent years to run faster on long steady runs has also helped my overall improvement. At college I was always being dropped in long training runs, although I fared quite well in races. But now I have come to the conclusion that my steady running pace of six minutes a mile was not pushing my pulse up high enough to give the maximum benefit, and by running faster I have noticed an improvement in endurance.

The standard of my interval running usually remains consistent, with the ability to run more repetitious at the same pace developing as I reach peak fitness. I run each 600-metre repetition in around 83 seconds, and 1000 metres in around 2 minutes 30 seconds or faster when I am fit, and I feel confident I can now run an interval session hard enough not to need the low-key races which some athletes use for training purposes. Another reason for my running relatively few races is that I tend to get very excited by racing, and if I run too many I might blow a gasket! So I prefer to run a limited number, but to put everything into them.

John and I do not use weight training any more, as we believe the acquisition of strength for middle-distance running is best achieved through the specific exercise of running; leg strength for that event is not comparable with the sort of leg strength achieved through weight training. When I did use weight training, it was only for upper body strength.

To accelerate recovery from hard training, and to try to reduce the risk of injury, I now try to have a regular massage once or twice a week, something which I neglected too often in the past, simply through a lack of time.

Now I try to make my training routine fit as conveniently as possible around my daily life. What I particularly like about running is that I can train for forty-five minutes, and all it takes is forty-five minutes, plus changing and showering time. I am not someone who likes to drive off in search of somewhere nice to run. I like to go out of the front door, and come back in through it as quickly as possible.

I used to run to and from work, but now that I need to use the car more in the course of my daily routine, I tend to get up around 7.30 a.m. with my young son Paul, make a cup of tea for Linda, have a couple of slices of toast for breakfast, then drive to work and run from there. My job as director of a charity which works in sport and recreation for young people in Coventry gives me a chance to do this, and having my office in Coventry City's soccer ground at Highfield Road means that I am able to use the showering facilities of the referees' room. I usually leave work at about four o'clock to run again, and then spend some time with my family. On Tuesdays and Thursdays I drive to Birmingham to train on the track at Alexandra Stadium. This year, though, I have the use of Coventry's new track.

I try to make Saturday an easy day, with two steady runs of about five miles each. During the day I do what anyone else does on a Saturday: shopping, mowing the lawn, or looking at all the jobs around the house which need doing, and then sitting down to worry about them. I do not race very often now, and I am not a good spectator, so I rarely go to athletics meetings if I am not competing.

Sunday is a more demanding day, with a traditional English harrier-style long run in the morning. I join a group of Coventry Godiva Harriers at 10.30 a.m. and we cover fifteen miles around the city and out in the country near Kenilworth Castle or the old Roman fort near Baginton. Sometimes we pass a nudist club, but no one has seen anything yet which has made us stop in our tracks. Then I go home for an hour or so and have a quick cup of tea, a light lunch or toast, before driving to Birmingham for an afternoon track session with other athletes coached by John Anderson, including marathon international John Graham and middle-distance runners Tim Redman, Lloyd Tredell and Steve James. Alternatively, I have a traditional big Sunday lunch at home and then wait until evening to go out and run a steady five miles on my own. Usually Sunday adds up to a total of around twenty miles, and the week as a whole to about 100 miles of running when I am in full training.

In recent years I have seen John at least two or three times a week at training sessions, although it has only tended to be a quick 'How d'you do' as we have to get on with the session. But we usually have a cup of tea afterwards, and try to set aside one day a week when we can sit down for an hour or so to chat about training and races. Although we telephone each other as well, there never seems to be enough time to discuss everything, and our opportunities will become fewer in 1984 when John takes up a new job at Southwark in south London. But I dare say we will find a way round it.

Right: Family group, with parents and sister Val, *c.* 1958

Below: Winning the Under-12 race at the Birmingham Schools League

The year 1970 was an important one and began with a Warwickshire road relay win for (left to right) Paul Eales, Martin Clark, Dave Moorcroft and Don Anderton

Four eventual Olympians fight out the 1971 Youths Inter-Counties cross country: Dave Black (210), Julian Goater (146), Dave Moorcroft and Barry Smith (75)

Winning the 1971 AAA Junior 1500 metres title from holder Ron MacDonald

Training with Sheila Carey at Meadowbank Stadium, 1972

Leading the Olympic 1500 metres final, Montreal 1976, from Wohlhuter (970) and bearded Frank Clement

Lasse Viren – Finnish Olympic champion, shrouded in mystique

John Walker (right) – an evergreen and formidable competitor

5

Olympic Baptism

The years at Loughborough were stimulating, tiring and rewarding. My athletics career made steady if not spectacular progress. In August 1973 I had made my 5000-metre debut in a Midland League race at Stoke, winning in 14:31; it seemed a long way. The following month I lowered my mile best to 4:01.9, finishing fifth at the Coca-Cola meeting behind winner Ben Jipcho's 3:56.2, and ended the year by being placed seventh in the England Commonwealth Games trials, which were held in late September to pick the team for the 1974 Games to be held in New Zealand the following January.

For me 1974 was fairly undistinguished; I ran in college matches and worked hard. In the AAA v. Loughborough match, in which I had first come to the attention of Basil Stamatakis three years earlier, I finished last in the 1500 metres in 4:04.1. There were other ups and downs, but I was working hard, training hard and investing in the future.

By 1975 I was on the up again, winning the AAA v. Loughborough 1500 metres in 3:43. From that I earned my first overseas race invitation – for a 1500 metres in Belgrade, in June 1975, which I won in a personal best of 3:40.7.

But a more important fixture was approaching. Linda, having completed her three years at Crewe, decided not to stay on for a fourth year for her B Ed degree, because she wanted to get out into the world and teach. I was going on for my fourth year at Loughborough, so we decided to marry that summer and live in Loughborough. Such domesticity would be a far cry from living on the campus, as I had in my first and third years, or even from the second year, when Terry Colton, Dave Driver and I stayed in digs with a Mrs Adcocks, who was the nearest thing to a saint on earth. She cooked us meals all hours of the day and night, whenever we came back, which she really was not supposed to do as she was only paid a pittance to look after us. It must have cost her a fortune, and we were all very sad when she died several years ago.

Our wedding day was absolutely unforgettable – it was the day Arthur Ashe beat Jimmy Connors at Wimbledon: I will always remember that anyway – on 5 July 1975. Dave Driver, who had been a very important factor in my development, acting as my regular training partner, was best man and we went for a five-mile run on the morning of the wedding. I did not manage a second run that day for some reason. Nor, I remember, would Linda let me go out for a long run with the lads on the Sunday morning.

In fact, I was in no state for such exercise, but not for the usual reason. During the Saturday afternoon and the later festivities Linda and I had deliberately stayed sober, and in the evening we bought some chips on our way to our first-night hotel. There was a bottle of Asti Spumanti waiting in the room, so we had the chips, the Asti and went to bed. During the night, I was sick. Next morning I had a hangover and a half. I will always remember Linda tucking into her bacon and eggs at breakfast while I was staring at a cup of black coffee.

Later that day we left for our honeymoon in Majorca and during that time I recovered, and actually got quite fit. I was training twice a day (what else was there to do?) and when we came back we spent the week cleaning from top to bottom the house in Beacon Road, Loughborough, which we had rented and in which we would be living for two years. We were scrubbing, sweeping, washing and working till the early hours every night.

At the end of that week I went up to Gateshead to honour a commitment to run a mile there, and succeeded in breaking 4 minutes for the distance for the first time. I

50

did not win (New Zealander John Walker was first in 3:57.6 from Mike Boit and Marty Liquori), but I was happy to be fourth in 3:59.9.

It was only a week to the AAA Championships, and it seemed as though despite everything I had come into form at the right time. I even got my first under-the-counter expenses payment at Gateshead – the princely sum of £5.

At the AAA Championships, though, everything caught up with me. I won my heat from the South African Danie Malan on the Friday night, feeling comfortable, in 3:40.5, just outside my personal best. Then I blew it in the final, which was won by Malan in 3:38.1, a championship record. I jogged in last in 3:51.3, a schoolboy time. 'Chokes me just to write this in my diary – never again!' was the entry in my training log that night, and the local evening paper in Coventry had a headline 'Sad Moorcroft flops in 1500m'. I cut the article out and stuck it in my training diary as a reminder.

Fortunately that was not the end of the season, and I was able to pick myself up the following week by winning the British Isles Cup 1500 metres at Cwmbran in 3:42.4. Three weeks later I won the Greater Manchester Mile at Stretford in 3:58.8, my best time, ahead of Frank Clement and four others who broke 4 minutes too. It may not have been exactly an Olympic final, but it did renew my confidence to be able to win the race from a good class field. All was not lost.

The summer ended with me winning a 1500 metres for Britain against Sweden at Meadowbank on a very windy day in 3:54.6 and being selected for a students' inter-national meeting in Rome, replacing the World Student Games which that year had been cancelled. I finished fourth in 3:42.6 in a race won by Thomas Wessinghage of West Germany in 3:39.7, and that was it for 1975.

Within a couple of weeks I began my build-up for the following season. In 1976 the Olympic Games was to be held in Montreal, and my every step that winter of 1975–76 was designed to help get me there as a member of the British team. I was running up to ninety to a hundred

51

miles a week, but every now and then there would be a cold or a twinge which would bring down the average, and nothing is more depressing than not being able to train when you want to. But you have to use commonsense too, because bravely running through a minor injury can turn it into a major injury, and running with a cold can set you back even further. It is sometimes more difficult to back off and say, 'No, I won't run today,' than to be sensible.

In January I turned out in the AAA Indoor National Championships at Cosford and was pleased to find I could still turn on some speed in the winter months, winning in 3:45.6, with the then little known Sebastian Coe fifth in 3:51. Athletics is a conveyor belt, with another wave of champions always coming through.

I ran the National Senior Cross-Country Championships for the first time at Leicester, not quite sure how I would fare over a nine-mile course. I was very pleased indeed to finish second to Bernie Ford, one of the kings of cross-country. The track season started well too with a personal best of 7:58.6 for 3000 metres at Loughborough in mid-May, followed a few days later by a personal best 1500 metres of 3:40.2 in Athens. That ensured that I had safely achieved the Olympic qualifying time in 1976. The Olympic trial race later in June, could be tactical, or it could be affected by strong winds. Either way, if you are going into a competitive race of importance, you have to be ready to run a fast time but not be over concerned if the pace is slow. Having the qualifying standard was a reassurance, and with my final exams at Loughborough occupying the second half of May, the Athens race was my best chance.

Once the exams were out of the way, there was no other barrier between me and the trials, which were to be held on two separate weekends at Crystal Palace.

The 1500 metres was held on the second weekend, which gave all those who had not made it at 800 or 5000 metres the previous week a second bite at the selection cherry. I was only going for the 1500 metres since I did not have enough speed to challenge for a 800-metre place, and the 5000 metres was not an event on which I concentrated seriously at that point.

All my training had been geared towards making the first three in the trials race. It was not a sudden-death trial according to the officials, but the athletes knew differently. With a maximum of only three places for each event available in the Olympic team, and half a dozen athletes having already achieved the Olympic qualifying standard, how else could they pick the 1500-metre runners if they did not take note of the first three home in a race designated 'Olympic Trial'?

My winter training had been good, the handful of races I had run that winter and spring had gone well, yet I had never felt so nervous, so paralysed with fear, as I did that weekend. This was the trial race for the *Olympics*, not some lesser meeting, and the Olympics are held only every four years. I was physically capable of making the team if I did not run poorly, or get boxed in at the wrong time, or fall, as I had done once in a junior international race in West Germany when I finished last.

That weekend we stayed with Paul Eales and his wife, Jenny, who now lived in Surrey. We had been very close earlier on, and I needed all the moral support I could get. One good omen, though, was that just before we left home news came through that I had obtained my BEd degree with second-class honours. So one ambition was achieved; now for the other.

In the heats on the Friday night, the qualification was stiff. The first five men in each of two heats made the final; the rest could pack up and go home; there would be no Olympics for them. I watched the bearded Scot Frank Clement win the first heat in 3:40, while among the athletes who failed to survive the chop was a fellow Midlander, Ray Smedley, who had been the surprise of the 1972 Olympic trials, going on to reach the semifinals in the Munich Olympics. But he would not be going to Montreal now. Neither would a skinny youngster named Sebastian Coe, who finished just ahead of Smedley in his heat. No one knew then that this Hallamshire Harrier, one of that night's also-rans, was destined to become Olympic champion in the event four years later.

My own heat proved relatively trouble free, and I managed to win it in a comfortable 3:43.7 from Irishman Jim McGuinness, while in third place was Steve Ovett, our top 800-metre runner, but very much an unknown quantity at this distance. He was very relaxed, even boisterous, because he had already ensured his place for Montreal by winning the 800-metre trial the previous week and was running the 1500 metres as a training run.

So then it was a question of waiting for Saturday's final. In a situation like that, where only three out of ten runners are going to go home happy, the hours are very long.

After watching the early part of the Saturday events on a blazing hot afternoon, I went off to warm up for the 1500 metres. While passing the back of the stands, I met Brendan Foster. He had just won the 10,000 metres in a world class 27:53.8, and would now be doubling up at Montreal, having won the 5000-metre trial the previous Saturday. It was five years since he had first ribbed me about being the youngster who was 'going to break four minutes tomorrow', but I still did not know him all that well, although we had travelled to a cross-country race in Italy together once, when he had clued me up about what really happens in such international events. But he stopped to have a quick chat, and really helped to motivate me. 'It's out there,' he said, pointing towards the track. 'If you want to get to Montreal, just tell yourself what a terrible Olympics it would be if you had to watch it on television when you could have been there. Remember that when you're running.' It was true, and I reminded myself that although I had been inspired by Brendan's running four years earlier, this time I did not want to watch the Games on television.

The race itself was decided on the last lap. Barry Smith led through the first two laps in 2:01.1, then Frank Clement picked up the pace on the third lap, so that we passed 1200 metres in 2:58.8. I was feeling all right and, coming into the final straight, moved alongside Frank to challenge for the lead. Behind us Steve Ovett had been badly boxed. With about 50 metres left a gap opened between Frank and me, and Ovett popped through into the lead. As he did so he turned to the main stand and waved both arms in the air in a gesture of celebration before turning back to win the race in 3:39.6. I was second in 3:39.9, a personal best, with Clement third in 3:40.

It was a great relief and a delight to have finished second, and with it came the virtually certain knowledge that I would be in the Olympic team. But Ovett's curious behaviour was somewhat irritating. To many people it looked as though he was waving to show how easy it was, which, if true, would be somewhat insulting to his fellow competitors. But he later said he was really expressing his relief, after having run such a terrible tactical race, suddenly to find a gap opening up to allow him through from the middle of the bunch, and he was waving to his parents in the stand.

Later, of course, when he moved up more seriously to 1500 metres, the wave became his trademark, but I always felt – being on the receiving end of the first of his waves – that he was such a good athlete, he had no need to do that. I thought it was going a little too far.

If there was one athlete for whom I felt sorry, it must have been Tony Settle from Sale Harriers, then one of our most promising youngsters. He had finished third in the 800-metre trial, after which he had been carried off the track on a stretcher suffering from a suspected slipped disc. He was back a week later, finishing fourth in our 1500-metre final in an Olympic qualifying standard of 3:40.4. He was not picked for either event in Montreal, despite having come so close, and those of us in the team deeply sympathized – there but for the grace of God . . .

That evening, with the feeling of an enormous weight having been lifted from my shoulders, I was able to relax a little. Linda and I wandered down to the fair at Coventry Carnival, and people kept coming up and saying, 'Well done,' which gradually helped it all sink in. I think even John Anderson, a confirmed teetotaller, had a glass of alcohol that night. All that year we had been thinking about the Olympics. Linda and I had been going without things in order to save up so she could go to Montreal if I made it, yet all the time I did not know whether I would. Now the sacrifices seemed worthwhile.

From this point, everything seemed to pick up. We had been talking to a friend of ours, Bill Lapworth, who was secretary of the Transport and General Workers' Union in Coventry, and I had mentioned that I was hoping to go out to Canada early to get used to the time change and the atmosphere. He said he had some friends in Washington, DC, and that if he could arrange for us to stay with them, would that help? We said, yes, marvellous, and although we still do not know how he did it, he arranged for us to fly out there two weeks before the main body of the team left for Montreal. In Washington we were very well looked after by Bob and Myrtle Myers, and were able to take part in the bicentennial celebrations of American Independence on 4 July, the day before our first wedding anniversary.

Then we moved on to Montreal, where I joined the team in the Olympic village and Linda went to stay with relatives June and Barry Holland in the city. As yet Linda had no stadium tickets, so we had to queue in a big department store from 6.30 in the morning to get some. The queue was long and at one point, after we had been standing for some hours, I had an altercation with a man who tried to jump ahead of us. A few thousand other people behind us added their disapproval, and he slunk away again. It was a great preparation for the Games!

A bonus was that my father's employers, Massey-Ferguson, offered to send him out to Montreal at their expense. They had run a competition among their employees for places at the Games, and I had drawn the winning tickets for them. They then contacted my father and offered to send him with the same group if he would like to go. He did not need to be asked twice.

The accommodation at the Olympic village was rather cramped, which was very trying for nervous, highly strung Olympic athletes. Five or six of us had to share one toilet and a bath. Each group had a main flat with five beds in it, plus several smaller rooms with one or two beds in each. We were moved around according to our events, so that those about to compete used the less crowded accommodation. Frank Clement and I were given a room together before the 1500 metres, for instance, and although we got on very well, it was probably not the best policy to put rivals in the same event in the same room. I cannot imagine Steve Ovett and Sebastian Coe wanting to share a room during the 1980 Olympics, for example!

In fact, for part of the time I did not sleep in the Olympic village. I would stay with Linda, then creep back into the village early next morning and ruffle the bed so that no one knew I had been absent. I felt that by using the facilities available to me outside the village I was relieving the congestion inside, as it became very claustrophobic at times.

The main stadium in Montreal was a huge building which would not have looked out of place in a science-fiction setting. Long disputes and strikes during its construction meant that it was still unfinished and the tall tower which had been such a striking feature of the original design had not been built by the start of the Games. Nor has it yet, eight years later. Even at the opening ceremony workmen were rushing round, hammering, painting, sawing, in a final dash to get the arena shipshape, if not completed.

I deliberately did not go to the stadium before the opening ceremony as I wanted my first sight of it to be when we walked in during the parade of teams. I am not nationalistic, but I love the pomp and ceremony and the music blasting out. It's exciting, and such an emotional thrill is available to relatively few of the world's sportsmen. I wanted to make the most of my opportunity.

A last-minute blow to the Games, less than forty-eight hours before they began, was the withdrawal of twenty-two African countries as a protest against a tour of South Africa (already suspended from Olympic participation because of apartheid) by New Zealand rugby players.

Whatever the rights and wrongs of the use of sporting events for political protest, the outcome was that the Games took place without such great African athletes as Mike Boit of Kenya, or Miruts Yifter of Ethiopia.

Dressed in our formal team blazers we had to wait for hours at the Olympic village before the opening ceremony, but at the time, in my first Olympics, I could not understand why some of the more experienced athletes wanted to miss the ceremony. Now I can, because it is a physically exhausting day of standing and waiting. Still, it was an experience I would not have missed for the world in 1976 as we marched into the arena to the stirring accompaniment of the music composed for the occasion by André Mathieu and Victor Vogel.

Competitively, my aim was to run solidly throughout, get through the first round, and go on to the final if possible. One's aims and ambitions constantly change, and there had been a time in my life when simply to run for Britain was the end of the rainbow; there could not be anything better. But once I had done that, it was almost a question of 'Very nice. What's next?' To compete in the Olympic Games was a similar ambition. After my selection for Montreal I was never happier. I had stepped up another rung, without having too much pressure put on me, and it would not be quite the same again.

The heats, semifinals and final of the 1500 metres were on successive days towards the end of the Games, from 29 to 31 July. The favourite was John Walker of New Zealand, who the previous year had taken the world mile record below 3:50 with his 3:49.4, and in 1976 had run 3:34.2, nearly 2 seconds faster than anyone else. My best of 3:39.9 ranked me a lowly thirty-first out of those who were competing in the Games, never mind those who were not.

In the heats I felt very good. Eamonn Coghlan of Eire took the lead in my race in the last 300 metres, and won in 3:39.9, while I eased up in 3:40.7 as the first three qualified for the next round. In my semifinal the next day I found I had drawn the favourite John Walker, the world's second fastest man of 1976, the West German Thomas Wessinghage, and Steve Ovett. The first four and the fastest loser from the two semifinals would go into the nine-man final the following day.

I was very, very nervous before the semifinal, which developed into a massive burn-up over the last 300 metres. I was back in sixth place at that point, and had to work very hard, but managed to move up behind Walker and Australian Graeme Crouch to third at the finish, covering the last 300 metres in under 39 seconds. Janos Zemen of Hungary was fourth, and Wessinghage, who should have been a medal prospect, went out in fifth place as the second heat was to prove faster. Also eliminated was Steve Ovett, who was sixth in 3:40.3. It was his fifth race of the Games, and he must have been disappointed as he only came fifth in the 800-metre final. But I must admit a quiet moment of satisfaction after the waving incident at Crystal Palace that I had reached the 1500-metre final and he had not.

The second semifinal was won by Coghlan in 3:38.6, having passed three men in the home straight, with Rick Wohlhuter (USA), Ivo van Damme (Belgium) and Frank Clement also making the final, together with the West German Paul-Heinz Wellmann, who was the fastest loser.

Reaching the final was, to me, like winning a gold medal. It was a very strange feeling because I had been so nervous before the heat and the semifinals. But before the final I was accepting everyone's congratulations and receiving telegrams as though it were all over. John Anderson was trying to get me psyched up for the race, but I was continually having to pinch myself to feel it was all real.

Even warming up for the final on the last day of the Games, I was thinking, isn't this great? I'm warming up with all these marvellous athletes and I feel really important. When it was announced that the 1500-metre finalists were on the track, I looked up and saw my name go on the electric scoreboard first as I had the inside lane.

It was like being given Royal Box tickets at Wembley Stadium. The gun fired, and I found myself reluctantly pushed to the front as I had the inside draw. Everyone tucked in behind me, grateful that it was not them in front, and I led through 400 metres in a slow 62.5 seconds.

Shortly afterwards Coghlan took over, but the pace was still quite gentle (2:03.2 at 800 metres). He picked it up on the third lap and was joined by John Walker as we approached the bell. It was obviously going to be a fast finish with everyone jostling for the right position. A slight gap opened, and the tall Belgian Ivo van Damme and I both went for it. He got there, and I did not. Instead, I received a nasty spike wound in the top of my foot, the scar of which I still have today to remind me of poor Ivo. (He was only twenty-two and won two silver medals in Montreal before being killed in a car crash a few months later.)

We were all running furiously down the back straight, and although I was giving it everything I had, I could not keep up. Walker went ahead with 250 metres left and kept a narrow lead all the way to the line to win in 3:39.2, with a last lap of 52 seconds. Van Damme was second, a tenth of a second slower, the same time as bronze medallist Paul-Heinz Wellmann, who had only qualified for the final as the fastest loser in the semifinals. Coghlan was fourth, ahead of the fastest finisher of all, Frank Clement, who came to life too late but finished fifth in 3:39.7. Wohlhuter of the USA was sixth and I was seventh in 3:40.9.

Immediately afterwards I was disappointed at the way I had run, and felt that if Wellmann could get the bronze then all of us had been in with the chance of a medal, including Frank. Only later, when the dust had settled, did I begin to feel satisfied that I had at least achieved what I had set out to do and gained a massive amount of experience not only of racing but also of the problems involved in day-to-day living in an Olympic Games.

The next day was something of an anticlimax as we packed our bags and prepared to come home. It was sad that the Games were over, but they had made me determined to come back in four years' time as a potential medallist.

But the standards were rising in all events, and even without the twenty-two African countries taking part, Britain had managed to earn only one athletics medal: the bronze of Brendan Foster in the 10,000 metres.

After the Games there was the round of invitation meetings, although the 'circus' was not quite as well organized as it is today. Within a week the Coca-Cola meeting was taking place at Meadowbank Stadium, Edinburgh, and although the athletes were somewhat travel-weary and mentally deflated, a sell-out crowd of 15,000 watched the meeting. In the 1000 metres I finished third behind van Damme, who set a UK all-comers' record of 2:17.5, and Thomas Wessinghage, who at least gained a crumb of consolation for not making the Olympic 1500-metre final by being placed second, ahead of me and John Walker, who was fourth.

To be fair, it was not really a matter of 'Moorcroft beats Olympic champ', because John had already made a detour to Philadelphia from Montreal for a mile race after the Games and only arrived in Edinburgh from the USA at noon on the day of the meeting. He always gives his all in a race, but that day he was pretty tired.

A week later at the AAA Championships at Crystal Palace we went through the motions again, as New Zealander Rod Dixon (who was fourth in the Olympic 5000 metres) outsprinted me with a 51.9 last lap to win the 1500 metres in 3:41.2. I ran 3:41.6, ahead of Frank Clement, with nineteen-year-old Seb Coe pushing the pace on the third lap with a 58.1-second circuit, and still running his own last lap in 53.2 for fourth place.

In Zürich I finished fourth in a personal best 3:38.91 when Walker won the 1500 metres in 3:37.8, and a few days later at Gateshead we both lined up again in the Rediffusion Games mile. It was a really blustery day, and Seb Coe (by now a student at Loughborough) set off as though it was quite calm. He opened up a big lead and on the third lap I realized there was a chance he might stay there, so I set off after him.

Walker seemed less concerned, and let me go. By the bell I had caught Coe, and we were 25 yards ahead of the Olympic champion. With half a lap to go I had pulled 10 yards clear of Seb and was doing my best to get right away from Walker who, nevertheless, had not given up, although he was still 20 yards behind me.

The wind battered us both, but the noise from the 13,000 crowd told me he was gaining on me, and in the finishing straight he edged past to win in 3:59.9 to my 4:00.4, with Coe third in 4:01.7.

There was one more major race to run in 1976. The Emsley Carr Mile, of which I had some unhappy memories, was being held during the British International Games at Crystal Palace on 30 August. Although Walker was not running this time, Filbert Bayi, the former world record holder from Tanzania, who had been expected to challenge for the Olympic title before the African boycott, was taking part.

Bayi was an uninhibited front runner on occasions, and had won the 1974 Commonwealth Games 1500-metre title in a world record 3:32.2 from the front, with Walker second in 3:32.5. Bayi had later set a world mile record of 3:51, which Walker broke with his 3:49.4 in 1975. But the showdown between them, so eagerly awaited in Montreal, had not taken place. So Bayi was now in Europe with something to prove, and it fell to Frank Clement, Brendan Foster and me to uphold the British challenge to him in this annual race. Oh, and Seb Coe, of course.

Coe hared off from the start and by halfway (1:59.4) had established a 12-yard lead over the rest of us. By the bell, Coe was still in front, but with 330 yards left Bayi led the chasing group past him and the race was on in earnest. Brendan and I chased Bayi round the final bend, and coming into the home straight I moved wide and got past him to win in 3:57.1, my best mile time. Bayi was second in 3:57.5 and Brendan third ('I'm hard to beat when there's a bronze medal at stake,' he quipped) in 3:57.7.

Coe held on well after his fast start to be placed seventh in 3:58.4 (the first eight runners broke 4 minutes). I had a feeling we had not heard the last of him.

For me it was a satisfying finish to a season which had been so rewarding in terms of results and experience. Yet although reaching the Olympic final was an ambition achieved, it was perhaps a greater irony that I had obtained my BEd degree with honours. I recalled how most of my schoolteachers had tried to persuade me to take an apprenticeship in the motor industry after I had failed all my O-Levels.

I was certainly a late developer, and I am not alone. I wonder how many young people are thrown onto the scrapheap instead of being encouraged to go out and develop their potential. It is my firm belief that many people are far better than they are ever permitted to discover.

6

New Zealand Welcome

When I came back from the Olympics in the summer of 1976, I felt that the experience had hardened me for the future, and that I could now compete with a greater confidence. I was really looking forward to the 1977 season. But all, it transpired, in vain.

In September 1976 I had started my first teaching job at Roundhill College at Syston, near Leicester, and towards the end of the year was invited to take part in a series of meetings in New Zealand. Although the New Zealand series is now well established for European athletes as a winter alternative to competing in cross-country or indoor meetings, at that time it was a new venture. Fortunately, I was able to get time off from school to go.

The journey out took forty-eight hours, leaving Heathrow at 8.45 a.m. on Sunday, 16 January, and arriving in Auckland on Tuesday, 18 January, at 11 p.m. stopping off practically everywhere en route. But it was probably the most enjoyable flight I have ever had. I travelled alone, as I was the only British athlete to accept the invitation, but met a lot of interesting characters en route. I started the journey with cricketer David Steele, who was off to India to watch a Test series.

Our first port of call was Frankfurt, where we had the chance to visit some of the incredible airport shops. For one moment I was tempted to spend the month there, and just pretend I had been to New Zealand, but I did not think I could get away with it. So I continued the journey, stopping at Tehran, Delhi, Bangkok, Bali, Hong Kong, and on to Australia and New Zealand. It was fascinating to think that I was flying over some of the most violent areas of the world. By the time I reached New Zealand I was exhausted, but my itinerary was such that in trying to miss as little of school time as possible, I was due to race the day after my arrival in Hamilton.

The top New Zealand athletes, John Walker and Dick Quax, were involved in organizing the series and I met up with them on the last hop from Sydney, where they had been competing. I introduced myself to John Walker, because although we had raced against each other a number of times, he did not really know me then. A group of leading West German athletes was there, including Paul-Heinz Wellmann, Klaus-Peter Hildenbrand, Karl Fleschen, Detlef Uhlemann and Michael Karst.

On that first morning they were all going out for a training run, so I joined them, which was a mistake. They were already acclimatized and had recovered from their journey. I had not, and when we came to a park I had to sit down on a bench to recover. I could not run any farther: my head felt as though it was full of cotton wool and the whirring sound of aircraft engines, which stays in your ears for a long time after a journey like that.

We went by coach out to Hamilton, where I was met by the 1960 British Olympic hurdler Vic Matthews, and his wife, Hilary. I already knew Vic because he had studied at Loughborough himself, then moved out to New Zealand to teach, but returned to Loughborough for a year in 1975–76 for an additional course to gain his degree. He was to billet me in Hamilton, as all the overseas athletes were looked after by local families rather than put in hotels, an arrangement which suited me perfectly. I was able to go to bed in the afternoon for some more sleep before the race without the usual hotel hazard of a chambermaid coming in to wake me up to change the soap.

As I was still so tired from the journey, the series organizers told me not to worry if I did not feel up to racing in Hamilton. But I went to the track anyway and thought I might as well give it a go. I ran the 1000 metres and somehow won it in 2:22.9 from Australian Ken Hall, Paul-Heinz Wellmann and local man Tony Rogers. It was encouraging that I could run that well in the circumstances. By the next meeting, three days later in Christchurch, I might even be awake.

I needed to be, because I was running 1500 metres against John Walker, who was coming back after an appendix operation following his successful summer. I was scarcely known in New Zealand, but when I managed to beat Walker in 3:39.8 that gave my name some prominence. After running the third lap in 56 seconds, I won by 2 seconds from Ken Hall, with Walker third in 3:42. The local paper, noting my lack of suntan after the English winter, described me as 'the Paleface Pom'.

Next day I won an 800 metres on a grass track at Nelson in 1:50.9 and three days later raced on the famous grass track at Wanganui which had been the scene of some of New Zealander Peter Snell's great miling exploits in the early sixties. The track was a somewhat disconcerting four-and-a-half laps to the mile, but not at all slow, and I ran a 1:58 second half to win in 4:02 from Hall, Quax, and the Pole Bronislaw Malinowski.

John Walker did not run in that event, and as I had won all four races I had contested in New Zealand, the final meeting in Auckland on 29 January was very much built around the two of us competing over 1500 metres. There were 30,000 spectators and they were not too disgruntled when Walker hammered me over the final lap to win in 3:38.1 to my 3:40.3. The organizers, too, were delighted as the series had proved a great success, attracting big television audiences and large numbers of spectators at the various venues.

The day after the race I played a round of golf with John Walker and his doctor, Lloyd Drake; during the game my back felt a bit sore. It got worse on the journey home to England. After a couple of days I started to run again, but was soon getting really bad pains down the side of my leg. It was to prove the beginning of a serious back injury which kept me out of competition for the whole of the 1977 season.

One decision had come from the trip, however, which was to mean a great deal to Linda and me. One of the reasons why I had accepted the invitation to go to New Zealand in the first place was to investigate the possibility of our moving there, even for a short while. It is a country which has a great running tradition, through Murray Halberg, Peter Snell, and then Walker, Dixon and Quax, and has always appealed to me as an attractive place to live.

During the first meeting at Hamilton, Vic Matthews had introduced me to Tony Hart, the headmaster of St Paul's Collegiate School in the town, where Vic himself taught, and I explained to Tony that Linda and I had been thinking of coming to New Zealand.

'Perhaps we can help you,' he said. 'There's a staff vacancy at St Paul's in September, and you can have the job for two terms if you like.'

He needed to know if we were interested fairly quickly, so I rushed to the phone box at a corner shop and telephoned Linda on a reverse charge call. 'How do you fancy coming to New Zealand to live in September?' I asked. 'It's a place called Hamilton. I don't know much about it, but it seems very nice, and the school which is offering the job is apparently a very good one.'

Linda, not always the quickest at decisions, said yes. So I went back to Tony Hart and said yes. And that was it. From the following autumn we would be living in New Zealand for nine months. It seemed too good to be true, it had all happened so easily and so quickly. Unfortunately, by the time I returned to England after the track series, I had the problem of my back.

During the rest of that winter, and the 1977 summer, I saw a veritable troupe of specialists and had all kinds of treatment, including traction. But there was no improvement. All I could do was to hobble around at school refereeing soccer matches and taking P E lessons. I could not run properly at all.

It was a very frustrating time. On the British international scene during that 1977 summer Steve Ovett moved up to 1500 metres, and won both the European Cup and the World Cup races. In the latter, in Düsseldorf, John Walker had run off the track at the last bend while Steve made victory look all too easy in 3:34.5, a British record. Meanwhile, I was shuffling around a football pitch blowing a whistle. And I did not even do that very well.

To make matters worse, I found that the British Amateur Athletic Board apparently did not want to know. Before the Olympic Games I had been included in the national B squad. When I made the Olympic final I was promoted to the A squad. But when I failed to show any form in 1977 because of my back, I received a letter telling me I had been dropped from both squads. That was terrific, just what I needed to raise my spirits. No help was offered, no one contacted me to find out what was wrong. When I wrote to the BAAB explaining the problem, they did not even acknowledge my letter.

So I learned that if you were running well, you were straight into *their* A squad. If you were injured, boy, you were on your own. Fortunately, things have improved quite considerably since then, though we still grumble from time to time. But at that juncture I had to make all my own contacts about treatment, desperately trying to find someone who was sympathetic and understood the sport, and who realized that 'rest' was not actually the answer I sought.

Eventually, it was Dave Bedford, a fellow international with even more experience of specialists' waiting rooms than myself, who put me on the right track. He referred me to Ken Kingsbury, who was then doctor to the British judo team, and he in turn managed to arrange appointments for me with several specialists, including an osteopath. I was X-rayed from every angle you can imagine (and one or two you probably cannot), and these finally showed that the fourth and fifth lumbar vertebrae had compacted. Once that was diagnosed, and I was

68

given the correct exercises and treatment to alleviate it, improvement was relatively brisk.

By September I had finished a most enjoyable year teaching at Roundhill College and Linda had given up her job at Castle Donington High School; now we prepared for our venture to New Zealand. To pay our fares we used a £1000 scholarship grant I had been awarded by Kraft Foods, together with our savings. We had a small amount in the bank which we had planned to use for a deposit on a house, but although everyone told us we were mad, we put it instead towards our single fares to New Zealand. We knew we would be there for at least nine months, but if my back condition did not clear up, we might be there much longer.

We arrived during the New Zealand spring; apart from the oranges and lemons on the trees, it looked just like spring in England. We were accommodated in what was actually designed as a bachelor flat at St Paul's. The school dormitories were built in a U-shape, with the teachers' flats at the ends of the U. Although the flat was very sparsely furnished, the staff were wonderfully welcoming. Three people had been round with flowers, there were cakes in the cupboard, goodies in the refrigerator and we were lent cutlery, crockery, anything we wanted. There were even hot-water bottles in the bed when we arrived.

We were very near the third and fourth form dormitories, so we could hear what the boys were up to. As they could also hear what we were up to, whatever we did, we had to do extra quietly! I would teach all day at the school, have breakfast and lunch with the boys in the school canteen, and Linda cooked for me at night.

We received free milk, bread, gas and electricity; in return we had to do two nights' duty a week when we looked after the house and I took prayers. We were also on duty one weekend in three, but the prefects generally looked after things and so the demands were not arduous. Linda found a teaching post at a school called Huntly, which was a large state school and a total contrast to St Paul's; she loved the work. As so many of our living

69

expenses were paid for, we were able to build up some funds again.

New Zealand proved to be a marvellous place; we never once regretted going there, we had such a warm welcome from the people. In addition, I was able to begin running again, albeit slowly, and became involved in the local Hamilton Harriers club, which gave me the chance to take part in low-key road races and relays and get myself fit. So in late September 1977 I wrote in my training diary: 'Commonwealth Games and European championships here I come. Watch out Walker, Ovett and Co(e). I am back in training. I have been waiting a long time to get going and the build-up has only just begun.'

The harrier clubs in New Zealand were something that I envied. Although they did not have the talent of the English clubs in depth, they were far better organized. Each level of the club had its own section, ran a thriving magazine, and was supported with tremendous enthusiasm. I still feel very close to them.

One memorable evening I met Geoff Dyson, who had been chief national coach for the A A A from 1947 until his resignation in 1961. He was something of a rebel in establishment eyes, but to many of today's coaches he is the father of modern athletics coaching. At Lough-borough (which he had himself attended) I had read his book *The Mechanics of Athletics*, which was, and is, the standard work on the subject. He was on a tour of New Zealand from Canada, where he was living and assisting with the organization of the 1978 Commonwealth Games, which were to be held in Edmonton, Alberta. I told him his book had helped me get my degree at Loughborough, although I admitted I had not really understood it all. 'Don't worry,' he said, 'neither did I.'

I was getting fit, enjoying my teaching, and although my performances in the second New Zealand track series early in 1978 were nothing special, I was working hard and knew I was on the way back. By the time we returned to England in May 1978 I was quite fit, despite one or two minor problems, and was looking forward to the twin

70

targets of the Commonwealth Games in August and the European Championships to be held in Prague in September.

In June I ran a 1500 metres in Florence, finishing second to the Kenyan Wilson Waigwa in 3:39.46, and felt that I was in reasonable shape for the AAA Championships later that month. I won the 1500 metres there in 3:42.92 from Amar Brahmia of Algeria (3:44.3), thus ensuring my selection for Edmonton.

On our return to England, Linda and I had put our names down for work as supply teachers; we were hoping to buy a house and needed a mortgage. Almost immediately we were told that there were two jobs available at the Baginton Fields School for the Physically Handicapped in Coventry. Neither of us had taught physically handicapped children before, and to be honest, when we first went there we were a little apprehensive. But within half an hour we really felt part of the crowd, and were soon absorbed by the enthusiasm and courage of the children.

Athletes tend to moan about every little ache and pain, but in truth we have nothing to complain about compared with these youngsters, who use their available abilities so constructively. Having taught in so-called ordinary schools, I have experienced the queue of kids before a PE lesson offering any little excuse as to why they cannot take part that day; most are pathetic. Yet at Baginton virtually everyone took part in something involving physical activity, and with great determination.

Even the most daunting illnesses occasionally had a lighter side. There was one boy there, an excellent swimmer, who had a serious blood disease which caused a dangerous drop in his haemoglobin level. Two or three times a year he had to have a complete blood transfusion, which would quickly make him strong and fit again. He always made sure he had his transfusion just before the Coventry Schools Disabled Sports so that he could perform at his absolute best.

Despite our initial apprehensions about teaching at the

school, we both stayed there for the rest of the term and went back again on our return from Canada in the autumn.

Although both were held in Canada, the Commonwealth Games proved to be a totally different experience from the Olympics. For a start, the atmosphere was more relaxed, and in some areas the standard of competition was honestly not that high. But all the men's middle-distance track events promised to be world class.

The danger during these 'Friendly Games' (as they are nicknamed) is that you relax a little too much and forget why you are there. But I found myself sharing a room with Brendan Foster, which proved a great help to me. He had accumulated so much experience since his international debut in the same Games eight years earlier that I learned a lot from him.

Since 1972 Brendan's attitude had always been my ideal, and I had long admired the way he could rise to the big occasion. So often talented athletes produce their best performances on the wrong day, but Brendan's ability to peak correctly was second to none, and one I have always tried to emulate, with varying degrees of success.

On the journey out to Canada I had a terrible time with sinus trouble, and needed some help from the English medical team in Edmonton. Brendan's encouragement at a time when I could have lost a lot of confidence was invaluable.

Linda came to Edmonton as well, staying with friends Fred and Polly Richter, and I was able to sneak out of the Games village and spend some time with her away from the crowded centres.

The 1500-metre heats were on 11 August and the final on the 12th. I qualified comfortably for the final, coming third in the heat in 3:41.47, behind Wilson Waigwa (3:41.4). But after the heat I was caught up in a set of those circumstances which can arise at a major games and may sometimes lead to upsets in the finals. I was summoned for a random dope test. This involves providing a urine sample under medical supervision. At

the time I believed that it was an instant summons –
do-not-pass-Go, do-not-collect-£200. The result was that
in my dehydrated state it took me a very long time to
provide the necessary sample. But, more important, I did
not get the chance to warm down properly, which is
essential for any track runner after a hard race,
particularly if he has to race again next day. Now I would
insist on warming down first, and invite the white-coated
attendant to jog with me. You are supposed to be kept
under surveillance to ensure you do not attempt to cheat
the test, or make a break for it if you have anything to fear.

I was perfectly happy to take the test, but less happy
about what the delay might do to my leg muscles. By the
time I had finished, it was getting late and all the buses
from the stadium to the village had gone. Linda was still
waiting patiently for me outside the doping control room,
and by the time we had arranged a lift to drop her off and
then take me back to the village it was about 11 p.m.

I jogged for a couple of minutes outside the wire fence
surrounding the village, then dashed into the restaurant
to get something to eat for the first time since lunch. By the
time I got to bed I was full of food, stiff and tired, but I
could not sleep. It was hardly the ideal preparation for an
important Games final the next day, but at international
level you have to be able to cope with this sort of upheaval
to your routine rather than let it overwhelm you.

As I lay there that night I thought back over the two
heats. There was no doubt from where the opposition
would come. Filbert Bayi of Tanzania, the defending
champion and world record holder, had shown himself in
good form and anxious to make up for missing the
Olympics through the boycott. In his heat he had stormed
through the opening lap in 57.1 and 800 metres in 1:57 to
break up the field. Scotland's John Robson stayed with
him all the way to the line in 3:38.8. Among those who
tried to stay with Bayi beyond 800 metres (and blew up to
finish ninth) was a gallant seventeen-year-old, having his
first taste of international competition, by the name of
Steve Cram.

In my more sedate heat Wilson Waigwa had won but given little away about his form. However, he had already run a 3:53.2 mile in Oslo that season, narrowly beating Bayi, and on the basis of that result most experts were tipping his fast finish to bring him the gold medal from Bayi, with the British contingent of Scots John Robson (who had run a 3:54.3 mile) and Frank Clement (a 3:54.2 mile) and perhaps me fighting for the bronze. John Walker was not competing because he had undergone a leg operation for compartment syndrome, an affliction I was later to know only too well myself.

Next day I travelled with Brendan to the stadium on the competitors' bus. He had already finished his competition with a gold in the 10,000 metres and bronze in the 5000 metres, but was continuing to give me moral support. He tactfully did not remind me that when he had run the 1500-metre final in these same Games four years earlier, also against Bayi, he had set a UK national record of 3:37.6 in seventh place! My own best time was only 3:38.9.

When I got to the stadium, I easily found Linda. She had paid 25 dollars for a good seat near the finishing line and had sat through pouring rain, getting absolutely soaked, bless her, so as not to miss anything. We sat talking for a while. I realized the enormity of the situation: here I was expected to reach the final and possibly challenge for a medal. It was not like Montreal, where I had achieved everything I wanted simply by making the final. My own hopes here were also high. I knew I was running well and yet the pressures were not as great as they could have been. Most people thought it would rest between Bayi and Waigwa, and so perhaps I could use that to my advantage.

I am not usually very coherent before a race, but when I said goodbye to Linda before I went to warm up, I remember saying to her, 'I think I can win this.' But as I spoke, I choked on the words, and my eyes filled with tears. In that moment, for the first time, I really did believe I could win.

74

There are always two agonizingly long periods of waiting during any major games. The first is on the day of the race, when you want it all to be over and yet the hands of the clock seem barely to move from the moment you wake up. The second is after you have warmed up, and have to wait with all your rivals in a small room under the stands until you are called out onto the track. It must be the nearest we come today to Christians waiting to be fed to the lions.

But the period of warming up provides a real relief and an outlet for pent-up energies as you jog in a world of your own. A few athletes like to talk then, but most just want to be alone with their thoughts and give little more than a nod to their rivals, even if they are good friends off the track.

When we finally got into the arena at Edmonton, it was a very different atmosphere from the Olympics: to me, anyway. It was the final day, and a capacity crowd of 43,000 filled the stadium. At the gun Bayi shot straight into the lead as expected and, as it transpired, Waigwa threw away his chance of winning by adopting the curious tactic of dropping right to the back, some 15 metres down on Bayi in the first 100; I was delighted that we had got straight into the race with a brisk opening, rather than having one of those reluctant affairs in which it all comes down to the last-lap sprint.

Bayi led through 400 metres in 57.7, with the Kenyans Kip Koskei and Richard Tuwei just behind him, then John Robson and myself. Koskei dropped back at 800 metres, but the rest of us kept in close formation, passing 800 metres in a fast 1:55.2, and on the third lap – traditionally the slowest – we eased only slightly. Bayi passed 1200 metres in 2:53.9, with Robson second (2:54.1) and me third (2:54.3). I only learned the time afterwards; following that fast opening 800 metres, I did not dare look at the clock.

With 200 metres left I sensed John Robson beginning to close on Bayi and I followed him, moving wide round both of them on the last bend, unaware that behind us

75

Frank Clement was making inroads on our lead at great speed. As we came into the final straight, I remember thinking, I've got a medal here, and when Robson tried to edge ahead of Bayi and I could feel that *my* final sprint was going to overtake both of them, I thought: it's going to be the gold!

But that straight seemed never ending. Eventually I was aware that we had crossed the line and I was still ahead, but one of the sadder aspects of modern developments is that nowadays there is no finishing tape to give you a physical awareness of having won. With photoelectric cells used for timing, there is no longer the need for a piece of white worsted stretched across the track. You have to keep reminding yourself not to slow down until well past the line.

The moment of victory in a situation like that is one of many mixed emotions: exhaustion, of course, but relief, excitement, and euphoria too. I had won in 3:35.5, with Bayi second in 3:35.59, just one hundredth of a second faster than Robson. Frank Clement had finished fastest of all (fourth in 3:35.7) and some observers felt that if it had been a 1510-metre race he would have been no worse than second. Waigwa finished an isolated fifth, a victim of his own folly in starting too slowly.

I was able to wave to Linda before being whisked away to begin the circus of events which accompanies a games victory. Bayi, Robson and I were taken to a protocol room, where a soldier explained what we would have to do in the medal ceremony. But I was so excited I took very little of it in. I just followed everyone else. When we got to the podium the medals were presented by Sir Roger Bannister, who, when the Games had last been held in Canada twenty-four years earlier, had won an epic race with Australian John Landy; both men broke four minutes for the first time in the same mile race. I was particularly happy to receive my medal from him.

Then we had to face the press, television and radio interviews, and the dope testing. This time I did not mind so much about missing the warm-down. Brendan had managed to smuggle Linda into the interview area and we were reunited in front of the world's press.

But amid all this I was reminded what a fine line separates success and failure. The 4 × 400-metre relay had seen a dramatic finish, with England apparently winning by just one hundredth of a second from Kenya after Richard Ashton had taken the team from third to first in the last 100 metres. Afterwards the Kenyans objected to an incident involving the third English runner, who allegedly had cut across their man. The result was that England was disqualified. Seeing how the team's elation had so quickly turned to abject disappointment, I was only thankful that my own gold medal was hanging safely round my neck. Yet it would have needed only one false step.

As I had not warmed down yet, and was brimming with nervous energy, I decided that I would run back to the Games village, even though I was not quite sure where it was. Nevertheless, I gave my tracksuit and medal to England official Barry Willis to take back to the village by car, and set off in the vague direction. Soon I met a dark-haired young Canadian running along, and we ran together. He turned out to be a leading local athlete who had been watching in the stadium and, inspired, had immediately set out for a training run.

He did not know me and we just chatted about the Games, until we met a group of England supporters who called out, 'Well done, Dave!' to me. He turned to me quizzically.

'When did you run?' he asked.

'Today,' I replied.

'In what?'

'The 1500 metres.'

'How did you get on?'

'I won it.'

'So you're Dave Moorcroft?'

'Yes.'

He fell silent. But suddenly I noticed the pace started to pick up. Whereas we had been jogging along quite comfortably, we now started racing along like demons, zooming through the Edmonton streets. It was almost a rerun of the final with Bayi now represented by my Canadian friend, and me struggling to hang on again. He got me back to the village, though; I am not sure I would have found it on my own. But that second effort seemed harder than the first.

As I wearily climbed the stairs to our room, I discovered Brendan had fixed a notice to the door: 'Congratulations, Dave – now wash your socks.' The Sock Test had been a standard joke between Brendan and me. Whenever we were going out training, we would throw our socks against the wall first. The theory was that if they stuck there, they needed washing. If they just fell down again, they were okay for another run. I peeled off my socks and chucked them at the door. They were still okay. But I couldn't help wondering how the notice had been attached to the door. Perhaps with one of Brendan's socks?

Later that evening Linda and I had a celebration meal in a revolving restaurant on the top of a tower high above the city and then went back to the village last-night party. It was the perfect way to end the serious part of the season, but that was not over yet. Ironically, the Commonwealth Games victory earned me selection for the European Championships the following month in Prague. Steve Ovett (who had chosen to bypass the Commonwealth Games) and John Robson had already been selected, leaving just one place. Poor Frank Clement, by so narrowly missing a medal in Edmonton, was also just a fifth of a second away from selection for Prague.

However, before Prague, I was committed to several more races. In Edinburgh, a few days after arriving back from Edmonton, I led all the way in an 800 metres to be overtaken virtually on the line by the American Tom McLean, but ran a personal best of 1:49.15. The next day I won a 1000-metre race at Coatbridge, and three days after that won the 3000 metres at the Rotary Games at Crystal Palace in a personal best 7:43.51, beating Rod

Dixon (7:44.92). Running the second half of the race in 3:43 gave me a great deal of confidence.

Two days later we left for Prague and the European Championships. Immediately, the difference in atmosphere and conditions was apparent. It was cold, wet and windy, whereas Edmonton had been warm and sunny for much of the time. Most members of the British team were still tired after Edmonton. Britain is the only country to be involved in both games, which take place on the same four-yearly cycle, so usually clash. By contrast, the Europeans, not having been at any other games, could concentrate on getting to a single peak for Prague.

The closeness of the two championships, and the difficulty of rising to a higher level of performance, was the undoing of many British athletes. Yet even those who had deliberately avoided the tiring trip to Edmonton were surprised by the standard in Prague. Both Steve Ovett and Seb Coe, who by now had become a world-class 800-metre runner, tackled the 800 metres in Prague, neither having been in Edmonton. It was the first of their direct clashes, and even after the semifinals no one suspected that neither of them would win. The only question seemed to be which one.

After Coe had led through an overambitious first lap in a stunning 49.3, Ovett came up to pass him on the last bend. It looked all over, but Ovett hesitated briefly, and a little-known East German, Olaf Beyer, came past both of them strongly in the home straight to win in 1:43.8, an astonishing improvement on his previous best. Ovett had the slight consolation of breaking Coe's UK record in second place with 1:44.1.

Beyer was also running the 1500 metres, and it was my luck to find him drawn in my heat, which proved a tough one as we not only had the 800-metre winner but also three of the eventual first four in the final. With three in each heat to go through, plus the three fastest losers, it was a considerable relief to get the heat out of the way. Eamonn Coghlan and I crossed the line together in 3:40, with Beyer just behind in 3:40.1, the same time as Thomas

Wessinghage, who therefore only qualified for the final as one of the fastest losers. I did not feel particularly good afterwards, so I had a massage and then went for a long jog.

Ovett won the second heat, and John Robson qualified in the third, so all three British runners were in the final.

Although it would be hard to beat Ovett, I felt I could give him a good race and at least stop him waving in the home straight. But when he went, as we all knew he would, with a furious kick over the last 200 metres, I was less able to respond than I had hoped. He covered the final 200 metres in 24.8, and although I managed to get up to second place in the home straight, he had gone for good, and I was edged by Eamonn Coghlan for the silver in the last few strides. Coghlan was pleased with second, but I was very disappointed at the time with the bronze medal, even though it did make me the only British runner to earn an individual medal in both Edmonton and Prague, such were the demands of the two championships.

Ovett's winning time of 3:35.6 was one tenth of a second slower than my time in Edmonton, while I ran 3:36.7 in third place. Robson finished eighth and the mysterious Olaf Beyer ninth, having lost form again quite suddenly.

I ended the season with a few more races, winning in Frankfurt two days after Prague over a mile in a personal best 3:55.3, with a 55.2 last lap. Then a 1500 metres in Bergen a week later in 3:36.6, and finally victory in the Coke mile at Crystal Palace in mid-September in 3:55.4, beating a field which included Filbert Bayi and Frank Clement. I was very tired from a hectic spell of travelling and racing, and so was pleased to finish with three good wins.

It had been a good season, with considerable improvement in my personal bests and the fastest 1500-metre run in the world in 1978. My confidence had gained a great deal, especially as I had missed the whole of 1977. Over the year I had established myself more firmly. Now it was time to go back to New Zealand for the winter to recover from recent efforts and to build up for what would, I

First gold medal! Winning the 1978 Commonwealth Games 1500 metres title from
Filbert Bayi

The stresses and strains of international running take their toll. This is the body of a very fit, but often injured, man

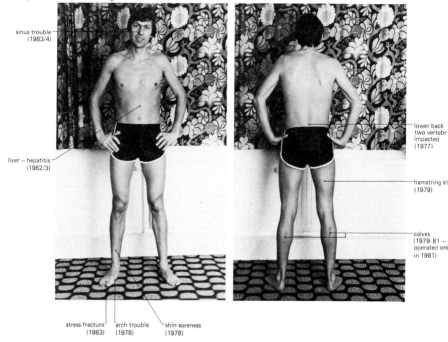

sinus trouble
(1983/4)

lower back —
two vertebr
impacted
(1977)

liver — hepatitis
(1982/3)

hamstring s
(1979)

calves
(1979-81 —
operated on
in 1981)

stress fracture
(1983)

arch trouble
(1978)

shin soreness
(1978)

With Linda and coach John Anderson after winning the Citizen 3000 metres at Crystal Palace, July 1982

Eamonn Coghlan is delighted with silver behind Ovett in the 1978 European 1500 metres; Moorcroft is less happy with bronze

Left: The anxiety and pressure show as Wessinghage (289) and Schildhauer (13) lurk ominously in the 1982 European 5000 metres final in Athens
Right: Striding out to victory in the inaugural Bannister Mile at Crystal Palace, 1979

Bill Adcocks — part of the Godiva history

Brendan Foster (724) — a great influence in the early days

Never happier than when helping youngsters to fulfil their potential, this time at a Nuneaton school

hoped, be another step forward in 1979. So the morning after the Coke meeting we went to Heathrow for the first stage of the journey via Los Angeles. The omen was not good, though. The flight left seven hours late.

7

Up in the Air

That winter in New Zealand was not outstanding, although my former Loughborough colleague Terry Colton travelled with us and worked as house tutor at St Paul's for two terms. We both suffered from illness during the season, and neither of us ran particularly well.

But the English summer of 1979 started promisingly. On the way back from New Zealand in mid-May I stopped off at Kingston, Jamaica, and raced a mile against the American, Steve Scott, who had already run some early-season races. When we crossed the line together in 3:55.1, I was not too upset that he got the decision because the time was still my fastest mile to date. He had led all the way, then I kicked past him in the straight, but he fought back.

Four days later, back in London, I raced in the first Bannister Mile at Crystal Palace during the Phillips Night of Athletics. I had been due to run 800 metres at the meeting, but was asked if I minded switching to the mile as they wanted as strong a field as possible. As it turned out, I was very pleased I did because I won it by over 2 seconds, in 3:56.53, from the Frenchman Francis Gonzalez. I led from before halfway and put in a 58-second third lap. It was not my normal way of doing things, but did not hurt my reputation at all.

The race had received a big build-up both in the press and on the night itself, with a host of Britain's sub-4-minute milers, including Sir Roger himself, being presented to the crowd. I felt an obligation to them to pick up the pace when it showed signs of flagging in the windy conditions. 'With a good winter's preparation behind him in New Zealand, Moorcroft looked stronger and more confident than I have ever seen him,' wrote Mel Watman, editor of *Athletics Weekly*. I certainly felt good.

Maybe my winter troubles were behind me.

But no such luck; they had only just begun. Shortly after the Bannister Mile I began to feel pain in both my calves. A distance runner gets used to various aches in his legs, but you get so sensitive to your condition that you can quickly tell if a particular pain seems especially ominous. This one did.

I had talked with John Anderson about eventually moving up to 5000 metres and tried one in Gateshead in June as an experiment. I won the race as a guest in an England against Scotland, Belgium and Norway match, in 13:30.33, beating Nick Rose (13:33.13) and knocking a chunk off my personal best of 13:58.4. This meant I had to keep an open mind about the 1500 or the 5000 metres at the Moscow Olympics the following year. But once again the nagging pain in my calves afterwards told me something was wrong.

I won the 1500 metres for Britain in the European Cup semifinal in Malmö at the end of June, with a last lap of 54.6 for a modest time of 3:46.3. But points count in those situations, and I felt I was doing my duty for Britain. I turned out in another mile on 8 July at Gateshead, but could not match the speed of the Czech Jozef Plachy on the last lap, which he covered in 55.0. He won in 3:56.8, to my 3:58.1, and it was sobering to think that he had been fifth in the Olympic 800-metre final eleven years earlier in Mexico City.

I was now also having trouble with a hamstring injury which needed treatment during the following week, before the AAA Championships in which I had entered the 800 metres for some speed work. I managed to win my heat there in a personal best of 1:48.54 and found myself lining up against such familiar figures as John Walker and Steve Scott. They, like me, were looking for speed in preparation for the prestigious international mile – the

83

IAAF Dubai Golden Mile – to be held in Oslo three days later.

Scott led throughout the first lap in 54.0, which was good level 800-metre pace for me, and I followed him closely past 600 metres in 80.3 and into the home straight. But in the final 50 metres I began treading water, and most of the field edged past, demoting me from second to seventh place. But my time of 1:48.60 was almost my best.

This rather faded into insignificance when compared to an astonishing world 800-metre record of 1:42.4 set by Seb Coe in Oslo a week earlier, the same Seb Coe who had so often in the past set a fast pace in 1500-metre and mile races, only to 'die' in the last lap. Now he had established himself as the world's fastest 800-metre runner and would be lining up as the 'joker in the pack' in the IAAF Dubai Golden Mile. On paper, ironically, he was the slowest of the twelve invited runners, with his 3:57.7 personal best, set when he won the 1977 Emsley Carr Mile. But few of us thought he would end up last in this race.

He did not. Following Steve Scott until just before the bell, he then broke away to win in a world record 3:48.95, to push back another level of unexplored territory. Behind him – some way behind him! – I set a personal best of 3:54.35, and rarely have I been so displeased with a personal best. I placed only ninth – it certainly did not feel like a personal best; it felt like a disaster. I was washed out, demoralized and, above all, my calves and hamstring were so sore afterwards that I decided to end my 1979 summer campaign right there.

I seemed to be getting nowhere fast. I had been picked for the European Cup final in Turin, but if I carried on the season I would be obliged to turn out for Britain and probably not run well in the final. I had experienced enough poor runs for the year. I wanted to get my legs into reasonable shape to be able to make a serious shot at the 1980 Olympics. I had already more or less decided on the 5000 metres, although I still wanted to keep my options open.

As an experiment I decided that I would try training at altitude. This method had certainly helped other distance runners in the past. The idea is that when you run at altitude, where the air is much thinner, your body produces extra red blood corpuscles to help carry oxygen. When you come down to sea level again you feel supercharged and run way above yourself as long as the beneficial effects of the training last, which is usually for two to three weeks. But altitude training does not suit everybody; I had to find out whether it would help me. If so, I would use it again in my Olympic preparation, as I knew many other athletes in endurance events would be doing.

In October 1979 the opportunity came to travel to Bogotá in Colombia, which is situated at a height of 8800 feet, and where Lasse Viren, among others, had trained in the past. The arrangement was that I would be flown out with Linda and stay there for a month, in return for running a 1500-metre race at half-time during a soccer match. It was not really a success. I ran in the race only two days after arriving in Bogotá, and just went through the motions, finishing eighth in 4:06, my slowest time for many seasons. Until you are acclimatized it is difficult enough to run at altitude, never mind race, and I had done neither before. Apart from the 1500 metres race, there were other events at the football match which featured leading international names, but the crowd could not have been less interested. All they wanted was the soccer teams to come back on the pitch.

There seemed nowhere in Bogotá suitable for training. We were staying in the middle of the city, and every time we went into the street we felt we were going to be run over by one of the maniac drivers or mugged. The people helping us were very friendly, but I needed more suitable conditions. When Viren stayed in Bogotá he had lived in a European community outside the city, and had special access to golf courses for training, which I did not.

Among the athletes at the meeting was the American Rick Rojas, who now works for the shoe company Nike and lived in Boulder, Colorado, which is also at high altitude. He suggested we might prefer to stay there, so we cashed in our air tickets and travelled with fellow runner Kim McDonald to Denver, and thence to Boulder, where there is an enthusiastic running community.

We stayed in Boulder for three weeks, and I managed some reasonable training, but decided afterwards that I would not pursue altitude training again. My type of training calls for speed work all year round, and one really needs a first-class surface to avoid injury. In Boulder there was an indoor track and a hard outdoor track, but neither was entirely suitable. Also it gets very cold and snowy in the winter, as do the few high-altitude venues which otherwise have good training tracks, like South Lake Tahoe.

It seemed that the warmth of New Zealand was still the best winter training ground for me. So we returned there during the winter of 1979–80, although for only four months this time. We were joined by Brendan Foster and his wife, Sue, and their children, Paul and Katherine. They rented a house in Hamilton and I trained with Brendan quite often. He knew that Moscow would probably be his last Olympics and wanted to give it a final fling.

I was still going through a difficult time trying to decide whether I ought to tackle the 1500 or the 5000 metres in Moscow. Obviously the 1500 metres world standard was moving on apace, but although I might never be able to match the pure blazing speed of 800-metre specialists like Seb Coe, in major games the strength to be able to churn out heats, semifinal and final often counts for more than sheer speed.

The wealth of 1500-metre talent in the UK meant that qualifying for the British team would be almost as hard as making the Olympic final. In order to relieve some of the selection pressure, the British Amateur Athletic Board in their wisdom had evolved a so-called 'elite squad', which allowed some of the leading athletes the right to be excused the normal selection trials. That was fine in

86

theory, but they then named *four* runners as 'elite' at 1500 metres – Ovett, Coe, Robson and me. With a maximum of three athletes per country allowed for any event, the term elite became a nonsense straight away. Later, they developed a new 'super-elite' level to which they appointed Coe and Ovett, leaving the rest of us with the prospect of having to run the most cut-throat of trial races, with only the winner standing a hope of going to the Olympics alongside the Chosen Two. So much for the preferential treatment of being in the elite squad.

All along, John Anderson and I had felt that the 5000 metres might eventually be my best event, but the question now was really whether I had got enough experience and training for the race during 1979. The plan originally had been to run more 5000-metre races to get to know the distance, but after the calf problem I had only managed to run one. Was it enough?

During the winter in New Zealand, I tried a couple more. In Christchurch in January 1980 I finished third in 13:29.4 to Mike McLeod and Henry Rono; then a month later in Auckland I won in 13:29.1. Both were personal bests, and I was reasonably happy with the results. I decided that I would go for the 5000 metres at the Olympics, but would run both the 1500- and the 5000-metre trials to keep my cards close to my chest. However, my training was now geared more to the longer distance. I was training pretty intensively on the track at that time, but had also decided that I had been covering my steady runs too slowly; running faster should improve my general endurance. Brendan was also training very hard, covering about 120–140 miles a week, but he did no track work. I found this a bit surprising because I have always run speed sessions all year round.

I came back from New Zealand with a bug which really laid me low for a while, but as a warm-up for the Olympic trials I won a 1500 metres in Louvain in 3:37.5 in early June. Then on 15 June at Crystal Palace I lined up for the UK Championships, which formed the Olympic trials that year.

John Robson, the bronze medallist at the Edmonton Commonwealth Games, had been forced to withdraw with an Achilles tendon injury, and Frank Clement, so close behind him, was also out with a virus. So the chief opposition would come from two youngsters who had both won gold medals in the European Junior Championships the previous year: Graham Williamson from Glasgow, who had run a mile in 3:53.2 at the age of nineteen, and Steve Cram, who had been in the Commonwealth Games in 1978 at the age of seventeen.

The 1500-metre final proved a slow affair (2:05.1 at 800 metres) and I was badly boxed early on. Fortunately no one made a break at that point. Williamson, who was celebrating his twentieth birthday that day, really picked it up from 800 metres, trying to drop the rest of us. But I followed him as he covered the section from 800 to 1100 metres in a very fast 41.7, and the penultimate 200 metres of the race in 26.0.

We covered the last 800 metres in around 1:52. I waited until the finishing straight before challenging Graham, and managed to open up a 1-second gap on the run-in. It was a struggle, but with enormous relief I crossed the line first in 3:41.5. Now the selectors could not ignore me for the third spot in the 1500 metres at Moscow – if I wanted it. But I was still no happier about the situation in which we had been placed. 'This makes the American system of first three past the post seem like charity,' I remarked at the press conference afterwards.

Neither Graham nor I had known during the race that Steve Cram had tripped and fallen as he tried to move out at the bell; his Olympic hopes appeared to be over as he trotted home last. However, he came back to run a very fast time a few days later, and the selectors ruled that he and Graham Williamson would have to have a run-off when I later decided that I did not want to run 1500 metres in Moscow. Cram won the run-off, and went to the Games.

My goal was now the 5000 metres, the trial for which was being held at Meadowbank, Edinburgh, a week later to give athletes a chance to double up if necessary. As so often in Edinburgh, it was extremely windy, so the times were not outstanding. I managed to outkick Nick Rose in the last lap to win in 13:41.8, and so was able to opt for the 5000 metres as my Olympic event.

If the selection problem was now out of the way, the calf pain certainly was not. Both legs were very sore after the race, and the pain did not go away until the following week. I was already committed to running a two-mile race at the Talbot International Games at Crystal Palace the following Friday against old adversary Filbert Bayi, and even on the day of the race my legs were still giving me considerable pain. There were now bruises where the calves had been bleeding beneath the skin.

In the first two laps of the race they hurt so badly that I even considered dropping out. But they eased slightly as I got more involved in the event. Bayi and I swopped the lead, passing the one mile in 4:06.9, which was on schedule for a time around Steve Ovett's world best of 8:13.5. But the pace slowed on the sixth lap before we finished with a flourish. I finally passed Bayi around the last turn to win in 8:18.6, a time which delighted me in terms of Moscow preparation, with the obvious reservations about the state of my legs.

A few days later I went to Italy for a 1500-metre race to complete my Moscow build-up, but a combination of sore calves and a stomach bug picked up out there resulted in a poor run which rather undermined the boost I had just received at Crystal Palace. If we knew in advance which races were going to be good ones, we would miss out the bad ones!

I managed to get over the stomach trouble, only to pick up a different, more serious bug when we finally reached Moscow. Brendan Foster shared a room with me, so naturally we both fell ill. It is hard to explain the frustration which accompanies a situation like that. You plan and plan, and train and train, and manage to get into the Olympic team, determined to make a big impact at the Games. And then everything goes wrong when an invisible bug gets into your system. The extremely unglamorous side of the Olympics is being up all night in the toilet, with your sleeping pattern ruined, your body jabbed with pain, and a weak, sweaty feeling which leaves you wondering if you can even make it back across the bedroom, never mind round an Olympic track at a world-class 5000-metre pace.

To harp too much on such misfortunes may often have the ring of excuse. But if you know in your own mind that you are fit, ready and raring to go, and then suddenly illness reduces you for one vital week to a limp rag, then there are no adjectives to describe how you feel. The more you have put into training, the greater your attention to detail, the greater the sacrifices made by other people on your behalf, then the more miserable the situation seems. Yet without that same input of effort and planning, you would have very little chance of success in the first place. In Moscow I drew the short straw.

Unfortunately, I was able to get very little constructive help from the medical side of the team.

'Don't worry,' said one doctor, 'it'll go in five or six days.'

'Terrific,' I replied. 'I'm competing tomorrow.'

I thought about asking the International Olympic Committee to postpone the Games for a couple of weeks until I was better, but they might not have been too sympathetic. So I ran in the heats and somehow managed to hold on to fifth place in 13:42.96 in a big dust-up for the six qualifying places, but I felt like death. I really weakened towards the end of the race and was lucky to survive.

Before the semifinals I had one day's rest and began to feel somewhat better. I was even able to eat a little. But I was not ready for an Olympic semifinal and ran very badly. I had not slept at all the night before and was sick twice before the start. It was a nightmare which I thought would never end as I saw my rivals pulling farther and farther away from me on each lap round the giant Lenin Stadium; I could do nothing about it.

Eventually, and I do not use that word lightly, I was ninth in 13:58.2, a time I could normally have run in training. It was little comfort that it would have needed a much better run to come even close to gaining a place in the final. In my semi, for example, Nick Rose ran 13:40.6 in fifth place and went out. In the other semifinal, Barry Smith ran 13.36.7 for *ninth* and was eliminated.

It was a strange feeling as a blank-faced official in a yellow blazer ushered me down the stadium tunnel with a sort of thank-you-and-goodnight gesture. After having devoted so much time and effort and been virtually a full-time athlete for six to eight months before the Games, suddenly everything had crumbled in a few minutes.

I went right out of the stadium to get away from everyone. At that moment I needed to be alone, at least briefly, with my thoughts, to get things into perspective. Within a few minutes, though, I was joined by Linda who knew where I would be and that I would need some moral support. We did not say very much to each other. We both knew what had happened and why, and we were each as disappointed as the other because we had both put so much into trying to get it right for the Olympics.

Within a few minutes I would have to go up into the stands to where my parents, Linda's father and uncle, John Anderson and a lot of other British supporters were sitting. I had to go and face them; there was no point in trying to gloss over the fact that I had not made the final.

When I got there, everyone was sympathetic. They all knew what it meant to me. But at least, although I felt ill, I was not suffering as much as John Anderson. He had caught the same Moscow tummy, but even more badly. He was drained and white as a sheet. He was so ill he had had to be detained overnight in hospital for observation. At least I did not feel as bad as he looked.

My immediate family knew there was little point in saying much at that point, but one or two well-meaning people tried. 'Well done,' said one. 'It's an honour to even make the team, you know.' I knew, and it did not help, but I was grateful to them for trying to make me feel better.

Unfortunately, there *is* nothing that can be said to an athlete in that situation which does not come out sounding vaguely patronizing.

So the Games were over for me. The Olympic history books will record I took part, and not much else. That is supposed to be the important thing after all (but try telling that to a disappointed athlete). At least I managed to see a little of Moscow, which is unusual for me as I am not normally a great sightseer.

I left Moscow before the 5000-metre final, which was won by the little Ethiopian Miruts Yifter, who had won the 10,000-metre gold medal earlier in the Games. I was back home in Coventry by then, watching it on TV. Linda stayed with her tour party until the end (she had little choice!), but joined me soon after the Games. In the time I was alone in the house I did some thinking and decided that once I was over the bug I would try really hard to redeem myself with some very fast 1500-, mile and 5000-metre races.

I never got over the disappointment of Moscow. I ran a personal best 800 metres of 1:48.37 in Nijmegen in late August, and was fourth in the Coke mile (in 3:55.73, behind winner John Walker's 3:54.4). I also ran disastrously in a couple of races, including the IAAF Golden Mile at Crystal Palace on 25 August. Steve Ovett won in 3:52.84, while I was only tenth in 4:01.71. Two days later, when Ovett broke the world 1500-metre record in Koblenz, running 3:31.36 (and perhaps trying to make amends for having lost the Olympic 1500-metre gold to Sebastian Coe in Moscow), I was way back in sixth place in 3:39.70. At the AAA Championships I stepped down to 800 metres again, but my 1:49.9 was good only for a non-qualifying fifth place in my heat.

Half of the problem, I am sure, was that the inner motivation was no longer there. I had always tried to develop into an athlete who could excel on the big occasion, and in that state of mind even the lesser races leading up to it take on their own special meaning. A personal best here and there at shorter distances can do wonders for your confidence as each piece of the jigsaw seems to fit into place. But once the big games are over, the focal point of the season is behind you. In 1980 it seemed as though the jigsaw had been completed by someone else, and I was simply left with a few pieces which did not fit anywhere. Perhaps 1981 would bring a happier season than this one, which had started so well, then fizzled out so disappointingly. I had to believe it would.

8

Release

The depression following Moscow was partly alleviated by confirmation in the autumn that Linda was expecting our first baby. As any expectant father will tell you, such tidings evoke a sudden concern that your wife takes it easy, puts her feet up, and is generally spoiled. For the first week, anyway. We probably were a little unusual, therefore, in our reaction to the news. We drove across America.

The trip had been planned before we knew the good news about Linda's pregnancy. Originally, we were going to drive with Terry Colton all the way to New Zealand (except for the wet bits), but because of the political problems in Iran, we settled for driving through the USA, where Terry would be running in the New York Marathon in October.

Naturally, we asked the doctors about the wisdom of Linda's taking part in such a journey, but they reassured us that all seemed well; as long as she underwent the routine checks in the USA, there should be no problem. We nevertheless took out heavy insurance, since medical bills in the States are no joke.

We travelled to the USA in September 1980 and stayed with our friends Bob and Myrtle Myers in Silver Springs, Maryland; while we were there they purchased on our behalf a 23-foot-long mobile home in which we planned to undertake our epic journey. We did a short trip up to Buffalo and Niagara Falls first to ensure that we could cope with the driving and camping, and all went well.

I was not running then, having been enjoying a break

after the Olympics, but the example of the highly
motivated and dedicated Terry helped to get me started.
We would train first thing in the morning, then have
breakfast, clear up the caravan, drive through the day,
and train again at night. Terry had always been
well disciplined at training and, believe me, you needed
to be in order to cope with such a tiring schedule.

We started our tour in Washington, DC, then went
round New York State, including a visit to Watkins Glen
where the US motor racing Grand Prix is held. Even Niki
Lauda would have had trouble keeping up with us and
our motor home. We drove on to Atlantic City in New
Jersey, and in early October we ran a 10-kilometre road
race in New Brunswick, which Terry won, with me
second.

In the New York City Marathon itself, which was
Terry's debut at the distance, he was perhaps a little
nervous. He went well for fifteen miles but suffered in the
final miles to finish twenty-ninth in 2 hours 19 minutes 15
seconds.

Afterwards we went down to Florida where we ran
another 10-kilometre road race, called the Bull Run, in
which I was second to the American, Ken Misner, with
Terry fourth. We stopped overnight at the headquarters
of Athletic Attic in Gainesville. Athletic Attic is a chain of
running stores established by Olympian Marty Liquori,
and he let us park there and plug our power supply into
his kitchen.

While in Florida we also ran on Daytona Beach, where
the sand is very hard. After Terry had covered ten miles, I
joined him for another twenty miles: ten miles up and ten
miles back. Afterwards my Achilles tendons were so sore
that I could not train again for three days. On the return
run we had to stop at hotels every three miles or so for a
cooling shower, because it was in the nineties.

We travelled on to New Orleans, and to Louisiana,
where the University of Louisiana at Baton Rouge has one
of the best all-weather tracks on which I have ever run.
From there we travelled on to Dallas, arriving in late

November and attending the annual ceremony commemorating the assassination of President Kennedy there in 1963. Ironically, and less historically, we were actually in Dallas watching the episode of the TV series of the same name which revealed 'who shot J.R.'.

We visited such evocative Western towns as El Paso, Tucson and Tombstone, where Wyatt Earp was so quick on the draw, and went to see Boot Hill, where those who were not ended up. At the University of Northern Arizona we tried out a beautiful indoor five-laps-to-the-mile track (oh Cosford!) and moved on to Las Vegas for a 10-kilometre road race for which the organizers tried to get us to pay 25 dollars each (around £16) to enter.

We drove down to San Diego, where we spent Christmas 1980, before moving on to San Francisco for the first of two races to which I had been invited by the American magazine *Runner's World*. The race was an indoor mile on 2 January; I finished second to Steve Scott (3:59.6) in 4:01.3. Then two days later I finished second again, this time to Alberto Salazar in the *Runner's World* five-mile road race in Los Altos. Salazar ran 22:04 to my 22:07.8, and both times were hailed as being under the 'world record'. Nick Rose was third in 22:13.1 and Terry ninth in 22:47.6.

We had decided that we would not go to New Zealand that winter, but return to England, where Linda wanted to have our baby. However we heard from home that the organizers of the New Zealand track series had been trying to get in touch with me because they had suffered a lot of late withdrawals from their meetings. I agreed to go to New Zealand just long enough to run the series of meetings, but we now had a logistical problem: we were still on the West Coast of America and our mobile home needed to be back on the East Coast, in Washington, DC, so that Bob and Myrtle Myers, the official owners, could sell it again. So we decided that Linda would fly straight to New Zealand from Los Angeles, and Terry and I would drive the bus back across the USA as quickly as possible. Then I would join Linda in New Zealand.

We managed to get the bus back to Washington in five and a half days, driving between 500 and 600 miles a day between us (and still totting up nearly a hundred miles of running that week). We literally did nothing else except drive, run, sleep and eat during that time, and it had its moments.

For instance, there was something wrong with the generator: as we drove it would gradually run down, and when we stopped and turned the engine off, we needed jump leads to get going again. So we had to be very careful where we stopped. Yet if we left the engine idling, it would charge up again. As neither Terry nor I were noted mechanics, we prayed it would hold out.

One night between Missouri and Kentucky we parked by a power supply for the van, turned the engine off, then found that the power was not working. We had no electricity and no way of starting up the van to move it late at night. We had to put on every item of clothing we could find and huddle in the freezing van for warmth. It must have been the worst night of my life. I did not sleep a wink for the cold, and couldn't stop shivering. We managed to get going next morning, and the following night treated ourselves to a warm motel room and hot bath – the only time (apart from during the *Runner's World* races) that we had slept anywhere other than the van throughout our 13,000-mile trip.

We limped back to Washington, only driving in daylight; because of the failing generator the lights had packed up. We drove the last three miles in the dark, though, and had to stop three times to let the battery recharge; it took an hour and we could have walked it faster. It was a great relief to arrive back at base again and hand the keys over to Bob and Myrtle.

Terry decided to stay on for a while in the USA, but I flew out to join Linda in New Zealand on 12 January, arriving on 14 January, but losing 13 January by crossing the International Date Line. It certainly makes for a headache when filling in your training diary. I won a couple of mile races in the track series (3:54.37 and

97

3:55.49) and ran as a guest in the Pan-Pacific Games 5000 metres, which I 'won'.

Then we returned to England, and I decided in complete contrast to take part in the National Cross-Country Championships, which were being held at Parliament Hill Fields in north London. I was very sharp from my track racing, and although the conditions were wet and muddy, and the course was nine miles long, I hoped to qualify for the England team for the World Championships in Madrid that month, in which I had never previously competed.

In fact, I had only run the National Senior Cross-Country Championship once before, when I had finished second to Bernie Ford in 1976. The start of the race is famous throughout the sport as being both an inspiring sight and vitally important strategically. Up to 2000 runners are lined up across a wide field, and when the gun goes they all sprint like mad to get a good position before the course turns into much narrower paths. Someone once estimated the first mile of the National is covered at a pace little slower than 4:10, with eight more miles still to go. Gaining a good position at the sharp end of the race is of prime importance if you want to do well; otherwise you waste a lot of time and energy overtaking other runners while the leaders are getting way ahead. If you want to figure in the race at all, you have to fight for a place at the start. My miling sharpness ought to help me there, I thought. I knew a fast start was vital. Everyone knew it.

You can imagine my feelings, then, when the gun fired and the field poured up the first hill – and I was still putting on my shoes. The warning gun before the start, which I had assumed was a five-minute warning, was in fact a *three*-minute warning. Thus, with some 1600 other runners having already covered 150 yards, I had to thread my way desperately through spectators and chase after the rapidly vanishing army of athletes. 'You've got a problem now, mate,' said one spectator with classic understatement as I rushed past him.

The race was held over three laps of three miles each,

winding round Hampstead Heath. By the end of the first
circuit I had somehow managed to get past all but about
thirty runners, accompanied by a chorus of remarks like,
'What are you doing back here?' from athletes and
spectators alike. By the end of the second lap, six miles, I
was up to twelfth (I later found) although at the time it
was impossible to tell how many runners were still in
front. I remember my old college friend Dave Driver, who
was having a good run, expressing his surprise at being
passed by me so late in the race with a remark which I will
not repeat here.

Part of the course was firm, and I made good progress
there, but the other half was wet and muddy, and it was
frustrating trying to run fast through it. I managed to
work my way past more runners on the final lap . . .
Bernie Ford . . . Ken Newton . . . Steve Binns . . . then
finally we had to turn right down a long, muddy finishing
straight and I overtook Steve Jones to reach fourth place,
with Mike McLeod just 2 seconds ahead of me in third.
Dave Clarke was second, while Julian Goater had
produced an astonishing run to win by nearly 2 minutes,
which is an amazing margin in such a closely fought race.
Needless to say, I did not see him. At the time he started I
was still taking off my tracksuit. By the time I finished, he
probably had his back on.

But although I was very annoyed with myself for
making such a mistake, I was still pleased with my run,
which told me that I was very fit, even if not fit enough
to be able to give runners like Goater a start.

Three weeks later I had a chance for revenge when I ran
in the World Cross-Country Championships in Madrid,
my first experience of the race. It would be marvellous to
say that it all came right on the day. But it did not. I
finished ninety-first of the 228 runners, and I did not even
miss the start. I can only put it down to the early effects of
a cold which started shortly afterwards, and the effects of
the mild altitude of Madrid, which many people had
overlooked. I had expected to run quite well, but it was
just one of those days.

Meanwhile, a new focal point in my working life was getting under way in Coventry. The story had actually begun some time before the Moscow Olympics, while I was teaching at Baginton Fields School. I received a call from the headmaster of Sidney Stringer School, a big comprehensive in Coventry, to discuss a project they had in mind.

This was a scheme to try to give youngsters living in inner-city areas a chance to fulfil their potential in sport, and I was asked if I would be interested in taking on the job of leading it. The post had already been advertised, but no appointment had been made. I thought the scheme was tremendous; there are all sorts of new social problems connected with the modern concrete jungles of high-rise flats, where the idea of running through a country lane might as well belong in a story book. But I was concerned about the degree of commitment such a job would require from me. I still needed to train hard and to travel quite often, and I did not think I would be able to work in a full-time capacity.

Then the Olympics intervened, but afterwards, when the process of setting up the scheme began, I was contacted again and asked how much time I would be able to give to the project, on a part-time basis. I discussed it with Linda; with the new arrival on the horizon, we would be staying in England instead of (as we thought) going to New Zealand after our American trip. So I agreed to become the full-time director of the Coventry and Warwickshire Trust, as it was called, from February 1981.

From the start I had a part-time assistant in former England swimming captain Pippa Jones, who also lived in Coventry. She had finished third in the 1980 Olympic swimming trials but was not selected for the Games as she had not achieved the necessary qualifying standard. But she had been a regular British international, having retired from the sport and made a successful comeback during university at the relatively late age for a swimmer of nineteen. Today, she and one of our colleagues at

100

work, Brenda Grace, are both members of the England water-polo squad.

To start our project in 1981, Pippa and I inherited a Duke of Edinburgh Award scheme, as the previous organizer had just left to work in Scotland. We also set up our own scheme, ACES, which stood for *A*pplication, *C*onsistency and *E*xcellence in *S*port. We had grants from the local newspaper, the *Coventry Evening Telegraph*, and were given a large cupboard at Sidney Stringer School which we managed to turn into an office, and off we went.

The aim of ACES was to give coaching and pastoral care to help youngsters from the inner city to become good at sport. But we were possibly too ambitious and naive in the early days in thinking that all those who were naturally good at sport necessarily *wanted* to be even better at it. You cannot make youngsters want to be superstars; it has to come from within. So we changed our aim, and now work at three levels: a bronze level, for all standards of children, and silver and gold levels for those kids who are giving greater commitment. But the project concentrates more on the fulfilment of potential rather than the production of top-line sports stars.

We moved office in early 1982 to the Coventry City Football Club ground, and our staff has increased to twelve full- or part-time workers. We operate what has now branched into three separate schemes, which interact to a large extent. We have the Duke of Edinburgh Award scheme. We have the ACES scheme. And our third section is known as the Recreation Industry Project, through which youngsters in the sixteen to nineteen age group can gain work experience and training in the sport and recreation industry while also improving their competitive skills. This was established with the Manpower Services Commission's backing because we realized that there were many youngsters keen to follow sport as a career but lacking either the academic qualifications to obtain a physical education degree or the talent to enter professional sport.

We have had our successes and our failures with all

three schemes, but it has been challenging, stimulating and a great deal of fun trying to help others make the most of their abilities in sport.

Early in 1981 my calf problem was going from bad to worse. I was struggling to train, but most of the time I was only able to run at a steady pace. I did some track sessions, but they were very poor, and next day my calves were always hard and sore.

On 4 May 1981, though, I forgot my problems and experienced the great joy of seeing our first child, Paul, born at 12.25 p.m. in Walsgrave Hospital, Coventry. He weighed 8 lb 2 oz, and arrived in one of those classic middle-of-the-night situations.

Linda had said before we went to bed that night that she was feeling some pains, so we had some warning. But in the early hours, unknown to me, she got up, dressed, had breakfast, vacuum-cleaned the house, put on her make-up and finally woke me up by saying quietly in my ear, 'Dave, I think the little one's on the way.'

Immediately I jumped out of bed and ran round in circles shouting, 'Don't panic, don't panic!' Linda sat calmly waiting for me, while I rushed into the bathroom to clean my teeth with shaving foam and tried to shave with my tooth brush. I was very brave during the birth though; I did not faint once.

It was, as I said in my diary, 'the most beautiful moment ever imaginable'. I even had the energy to run four miles later that day, and next morning, in between hospital visits, I covered five miles. 'Beautiful morning and I really enjoyed the run . . . feel light as a feather,' I wrote.

Unfortunately, I was feeling as light as a lead balloon by the time of the IAAF Golden 5000 Metres at Gateshead a month later, the first time young Paul was taken to an athletics meeting. Well, it had to happen some time. The race was won by Barry Smith, who lived locally and ran for Gateshead Harriers in the footsteps of Brendan Foster. It was an exciting moment for the big crowd to see a classy international field defeated by the local man in 13:21.14. My own part in the race was not exactly brilliant: I wound up thirteenth (in 13:37.51), feeling terrible; once I start running badly, I make a good job of it. Afterwards, more worryingly, my calves were very sore.

I had already been selected to run 1500 metres for Britain against East Germany in Dresden the following week, and I felt it was important to take part to try to regain some confidence. The British team had another nightmare journey there, arriving exhausted in the middle of the night. So I was pleasantly surprised at being able to outkick the European 800-metre champion Olaf Beyer in the relatively slow time of 3:46.89, with a 54.0 last lap.

My legs were still giving me pain. The problem had by now been diagnosed as compartment syndrome, in which the sheaths which enclose the calf muscles are too tight for the expanding muscles, hence the pain. An operation can be performed to split the sheaths, and it was this operation which other athletes like Mary Decker and John Walker underwent, which allowed them to continue their careers successfully after suffering from the same problem. A similar operation seemed the perfect solution for me. The question was when. The surgeon suggested that it would be helpful to examine me shortly after a hard race, when my legs would still be painful.

I had been offered a 5000-metre race in Lausanne, so I accepted the invitation, intending to run and then return for the operation. But to my surprise I won the race in a personal best of 13:20.51, beating the new European 10,000-metre record holder Fernando Mamede of Portugal. This changed everything. At the very time I was preparing to abort the season for the operation, the British selectors suddenly started to have confidence in me. As a result of my win in Lausanne (and perhaps also a 3:54.93-mile in Louvain shortly before that) I was selected as the British representative for the 5000 metres in the European Cup final in Zagreb on 16 August. However, Barry Smith, who had not only won the I A A F

Golden 5000 Metres but also the 5000 metres for Britain in the European Cup semifinal in Helsinki, was being dropped for the final. He had done nothing wrong, yet the selectors apparently felt he lacked sufficient pace for the likely fast finish in Zagreb.

This was a little bit embarrassing. Although it was not a problem of my making, I felt great sympathy for Barry, but I had so often felt the rough end of the selectors' decisions that it was a pleasant change to receive their confidence this time. 'It was a desperately difficult decision for the selectors to come to,' said Frank Dick, the U K Director of Coaching at a press conference. 'Barry has shown us that he can run a very sound tactical race providing the pressure is on for the last two kilometres.'

I was under tremendous win-or-nothing pressure as a result of the selection. It was very hot in Zagreb, and the pace of the 5000 metres proved to be very gentle. I stayed at the back early on, but as the final kilometre approached, I moved up to the front with three laps left.

I stayed there as we picked up speed approaching the bell, and hugged the inside lane all the way round the final lap, holding off Hansjörg Kunze of East Germany and Valeriy Abramov of the USSR in a last lap of 54.03 seconds, with the final 200 metres taking 25.5. My overall time of 13:43.18 was less than sensational, but I was pleased (and relieved) to win and thus secure the maximum points for Britain. We eventually finished third in the team event, our best placing ever.

Then came another quirk of fate. I hoped that after winning in Zagreb I would be picked for the European Select team at the World Cup in Rome the following month. In the World Cup the two leading teams from the European Cup (East Germany and the USSR in 1981) take part as separate units, with a third composite team, Europe Select, made up of other European athletes. The three European squads compete with five other teams, representing Asia, Oceania, the USA, the Americas and Africa. There is one man per event, and every event is a straight final.

However, when the Europe Select team was announced, the single 5000-metre spot went to Eamonn Coghlan of Eire, who had run slightly faster than my best time, but was not running in the European Cup final race because Eire had not qualified as a team. What annoyed me (apart from the fact that I had already postponed my calf operation until 7 September, the day after the World Cup race) was not so much that he had been chosen over me, but that he had apparently been told that he had been pencilled into the team *before* the Zagreb race. Presumably no matter how fast I had run there, I would still not have been picked for the World Cup. I felt very bitter about that, although Eamonn produced the goods in the World Cup, winning the race for the Europe Select team in a tactical 14:08.39.

My own finish to the season was much more downbeat, unfortunately, as I contracted a throat infection and my last two races were disappointments. It was that time in August 1981 when Steve Ovett and Sebastian Coe swopped the world mile record between them three times in nine days. I happened to be in Steve's race at Koblenz, where he ran 3:48.40 to break Seb Coe's mark of 3:48.53 in Zürich a week earlier. But Seb reclaimed it two days later with 3:47.33 in Brussels. It was an astonishing chapter in middle-distance running history.

I had finished fourth in Koblenz in 4:00.55, then went on a complicated journey to Ardal in Norway, via seaplane and ferry, to run 1500 metres in an England–Norway–Yugoslavia international match. Ardal is a lovely town in the fjordland of Norway, but I felt really ill and finished last in 3:50.

It had been a strange season with its fair share of misfortune: the missed start at the National Cross-Country, the awful 5000-metre run at Gateshead, and all the time those tight, aching calves – both legs felt as though they were continually clamped in a vice – from which I could find no relief.

It was with both trepidation and enthusiasm that on 6 September I went into St Gerard's Hospital, Coleshill (between Coventry and Birmingham). It is a beautiful place, run by wonderfully dedicated nuns, with whom I still correspond, particularly Sister Brigid. I was in there a week for that operation to split the sheaths of my calf muscles. Ironically, I was actually having my legs shaved for the operation at the exact moment Eamonn Coghlan was winning in Rome, and I was able to see the race on TV at the same. While I was in the hospital I enjoyed the company of some of the other lads who were recovering from various leg operations, but I was pleased to be able to get out and become active again.

When the stitches were removed, I went with Linda, baby Paul and my parents to Clearwater, near Tampa in Florida, for a holiday, and within three or four weeks of the operation, I began running again. Although my legs were weak, they felt distinctly different, and with my gradually returning fitness came the full realization that the pain had finally gone.

By November I was ready to run on the track again. I was terrified in case the pain came back, to dash all my renewed hopes, but my legs were fine, no trouble at all, and I was able to get in a good period of training up to Christmas. I ran a four-and-a-half-mile road race in Ipswich just before Christmas and broke the course record by 50 seconds, then on Boxing Day flew to Zürich for a five-mile road race just before the New Year. It was a marvellous Christmassy atmosphere there, very, very cold, snow on the ground and huge crowds. I won the race by half a minute from a good field, which was encouraging.

In the New Year we made our traditional New Zealand visit and I managed to get in a sustained period of 100-miles-a-week training, including lots of trackwork, some of it in Auckland with a good friend, Tony Rogers. I felt I was really flying along.

In late January I even managed to run several sub-4-minute miles, and in one seven-day period I won two fast 5000-metre races, with a 3000 metres sandwiched in between. None produced leg problems. With the

European Championships due to be held in Athens in September, and the Commonwealth Games in Brisbane in October, I could now confidently hope to be able to run 5000 metres in both with no recurrence of the calf trouble. It was a wonderful feeling to be able to plan ahead again and no longer have to worry about how much work my legs would let me do.

We came back to England in time for the National Cross-Country Championships which were held that year in Leeds. I caused a major sensation by actually getting to the start on time, but did not feel too good in the race itself. I had been suffering from a stomach problem which manifested itself as a stitch every time I ran. In fact I nearly did not race at all. But Coventry Godiva Harriers were fielding a particularly strong team and I wanted to help them out.

Strangely, although I had joined Godiva during their golden years when Dick Taylor, Basil Heatley and Bill Adcocks were running for them, I had never actually been a part of that success. When I made my own international breakthrough, the club was going through some lean patches, and it was only in the early eighties that the nucleus of a similarly strong team began to develop. That day at Leeds we finished second in the team race, and I was fourth individually, behind Dave Clarke, Hugh Jones and Mike McLeod. It still remains an ambition to help Godiva win the National team title, and of course to win the individual title myself.

Although I had qualified for the World Cross-Country Championships, I later withdrew from the England team because my stomach trouble had still not cleared up. But by the time of the A A A National twelve-stage road relay in April, on its traditional course at Sutton Coldfield, I was as fit as I have ever been.

It was one of those days when I sensed I was going to run well. That week I had achieved a training session of 5 × 1000 metres in 2:29, 2:28, 2:28, 2:27 and 2:28 with a 1000-metre jog in six minutes as recovery in between. When Lloyd Tredell handed over to me in twelfth place (having himself made up eight places on the second leg), I had eleven runners spread out 50 seconds in front of me and five and a half miles in which to catch them. It could not have been set up better, and I felt I could run faster and faster. By the time I handed over to Dave Smith at the end of my leg, we were 46 seconds ahead of the field and it transpired that I had broken Brendan Foster's course record, set in 1974, with 24 minutes 27 seconds. Remembering how well Brendan had been running in 1974, when he broke the world 3000-metre record and easily won the European 5000-metre title, it was a pleasing indication of my own form, especially as the record had withstood attack for so long. Coventry was finally placed seventh in the race, but I was more than satisfied with my own run.

In May I went out briefly to the USA to run in the Revco 10-kilometre road race, which I won in 28:04. But during the race I hurt the back of my leg and on my return home had to miss the start of the UK track season.

Eventually my first race was at Gateshead on 13 June, where I won a 3000 metres in the U-Bix Copiers international meeting in 7:52.5. With new-found confidence, I took the lead just after halfway and was able to win by running the last kilometre in 2:29.5 and the last lap in 55.9, to hold off the Kenyan Wilson Waigwa. Although the overall time was not fast, the race told me I was back where I wanted to be. Afterwards, in answer to questions from journalists, I said that I would not be racing much that summer 'because it is so important to get it right in September and October', when the European and Commonwealth Games were to be held. All I was planning beforehand were two visits to Oslo, for a mile and a 5000 metres, and a 3000 metres at Crystal Palace on 17 July in which Sydney Maree, Steve Scott, Steve Ovett and Seb Coe were all due to run.

It seemed as though everything was going perfectly in my build-up to the big games. In training I was churning out fast repeat sessions of 600-metre and 1000-metre interval runs, and almost begging John for more. In early

108

June I ran 4 × 600 metres in 85.0, 83.3, 83.4, and 82.6 with just a 600-metre jog in between. It was my best session ever, and I was in the form of my life.

Yet, curiously, I was unhappy and disturbed inside. I have thought about it a lot since, and although I still do not know whether it was cause and effect, I do know that while I was on the running track I could reach down to a new level of intensity which I had never before approached. But in my own mind and in my everyday life, I was going through an uncharacteristic turmoil which is almost frightening to recall now.

9

13:00.41

Sometimes we have to ask ourselves *why*. For the distance runner there has to be some inner drive which keeps you going out of the front door to train on wet, cold nights when your commonsense tells you it would be much more comfortable to sit by the fire and watch television. Usually we say it is because we are 'competitive' or we 'enjoy feeling fit', and that is certainly true to some extent.

But it has to be more than that. Unlike some athletes, I am not intensely competitive in everything. There are those who always have to win, even if it is only a game of cards. Not me. If I play golf and fluff a shot, I think it is funny. But I know some other athletes who would probably throw down their clubs in a rage. I am not saying that is a bad attitude, but it is not *my* attitude.

On the track, though, I am intensely competitive. Although I like to think that I can still lose courteously, I do not consider the next man's feelings if I can beat him in a race. Afterwards, though, we are mates again.

But early in 1982 my attitude changed. Never have I felt so masochistic and aggressive in my training. It coincided with a period when both Linda and John noticed that I seemed to have changed my personality. For a span of between three and six months for some reason I was not a particularly pleasant person. I felt very frustrated at that time, but the change which came over me was both quite uncharacteristic and, in retrospect, puzzling.

John noticed it in training. I would turn up for the usual track sessions on Tuesday and Thursday nights at

Alexandra Stadium, Birmingham, get straight on with warming-up, then do the session, usually at a very high intensity, warm down, shower, and go home with scarcely a word to anyone. John was delighted I was running so well but was concerned that our usually relaxed, friendly relationship seemed threatened for some unknown reason.

Linda, too, tells me now how concerned she was at the time. I seemed to be behaving so oddly, like driving the car at nearly 100 m.p.h. on the motorway whenever possible and being moody and taciturn at home. When we visited friends, or even relatives, I would stay in a corner hardly speaking; at one party I was silent most of the evening, which resulted in Linda having to chatter away nineteen to the dozen to cover up for me.

Looking back, it seems as though it was a different person, not me. But at the time I was in a strange state of mind. I genuinely did not care what happened, yet I was taking everything out on myself in training. I was putting 101 per cent effort into every run, then going back for more. It was almost as if I was punishing myself, or taking solace in the one thing in which I did not find frustration. The A A A National road relay came during that period. I was really wound up and felt very near breaking point that day, yet as a performance the run I achieved was possibly as good as anything I have ever done.

It is hard to unravel the causes. So far as running went, it may have been brought about by a fear of finally having to face my destiny. For much of my career there had been setbacks and problems. In the early days I could always shrug aside such things as I was still young and learning. More recently, there had usually been some comfortable excuse on which to fall back: the stomach bug in Moscow, the aching calves which would not function properly.

But that was no longer the case. At last, I had no physical ailments. I had a good winter behind me. I was running brilliantly in training. And I was twenty-nine years old. I had to face up to the fact that this was the moment of truth, and perhaps I was scared of failure, of discovering that, after all, I could not do it simply because I could not do it.

Perhaps I was training like a lunatic just to try to minimize the chance of failure, whatever that constituted. I felt like a parachutist about to step out of an aeroplane for the first time. I had been through the mock jumps, and the jumps from towers attached to safety harnesses. But this time it was real. And I felt terrified.

I experienced excitement and fear, with adrenalin constantly flowing; I was working long hours, scarcely able to sit still for a second, restlessly prowling in search of activity of one sort or another which would alleviate this great gnawing frustration. There was tension at home as I tried to ignore the strain I was putting on Linda with my moodiness. She found some solace in Paul, and in all honesty I do not believe it was a jealousy of our new son that brought about the change. I felt nothing but pride and devotion towards him.

Yet there has to be some other explanation. Why, for example, did it matter so much to me to run well? It always had done, of course, but at that time the need seemed so acute, almost animalistic in the way I was training. I could understand how a professional boxer who had perhaps been dragged up in tough surroundings might desperately need to win for the sake of survival. The hungriest fighters are the toughest. But in someone who was brought up in reasonable comfort, and had a house, family and job he enjoyed, it seemed less than logical. Perhaps through competition I would find out.

On 25 June I travelled to Oslo for the first of my two planned races there. It was a mile against the Americans, Steve Scott and Sydney Maree, and although I did not expect to win in such company, I was hoping to improve my previous best time of 3:54.4 set in that disastrous Golden Mile in 1979. The day before the race I attended the famous strawberry party which is held in the garden of meeting promoter Arne Haukvik before each Oslo gathering, and that evening my hotel room-mate Bill Hartley and I met up with Cliff Temple for dinner near

The frustration of the Moscow Olympics as John Treacy (409) leads the 5000 metres semifinal

Above: Still unable to believe the performance, but acknowledging the crowd's applause after the world record; Oslo, July 1982

Left: A moment to remember — the world 5000 metres record in Oslo, 13 minutes 20.41 seconds

After the world record, everyone wanted a word. And this was just the beginning

Celebrating the award of the MBE, June 1983, with Linda and Paul

A happier end to 1982 — victory at the Brisbane Commonwealth Games

the famous Bislett Stadium. Afterwards the three of us walked around the stadium, and I was very disappointed to see it looking so lifeless. My brief memory of it from 1979 was of being on the track, with the thousands of spectators so close to the competitors. To see it practically deserted was like walking through an empty theatre. Now it just looked tatty. There were graffiti sprayed on the outside of the walls, and the hyper-fast track on which so many records had been set was, on close inspection, patched and heavily repaired.

Yet the next night, when the stands were packed with spectators pressed up against the edge of the six-lane track, the Bislett magic came alive again. Urged on by Arne Haukvik, who walked up and down the home straight with a small loudhailer urging the crowd to cheer more frantically, the spectators chanted through the distance races and practically carried the athletes to fast times on sheer noise. The red-brown track, for all its repairs, was still clearly superfast.

In our mile Englishman Bob Benn (54.8 at 440 yards) and Australian Pat Scamell (880 yards in 1:53 and three-quarters of a mile in 2:53.9) undertook the pacemaking. On the last lap Steve Scott outsprinted Sydney Maree in an American record of 3:48.53, becoming the third fastest miler ever after Coe and Ovett. Maree ran 3:48.83, while I was delighted with third place in 3:49.34, which took some 5 seconds off my personal best, just ahead of John Walker, whose 3:49.50 was only one tenth slower than his world record set seven years earlier.

With a sub-3:50 time to my credit I could at last call myself a miler; it was ironic that only after I had moved up to 5000 metres did I finally make such an improvement in the mile. It also confirmed my feeling that I was at last beginning to reach the level of performance of which I had felt capable, but had in the past never been able to reach.

Back home I seemed to be coming out of my black depression, but I still felt somewhat confused and unsettled in my everyday life. That time was the closest I had ever been to believing that you have to be nasty to win, and that nice guys only come second.

John was naturally delighted with my mile time, especially as a track session in Birmingham just before I had left for Oslo had turned out disastrously. I was supposed to have run 4 × 600 metres, but after warming up I felt absolutely psyched out and could not tackle the session. John realized I was not messing around. I had pulled out of sessions occasionally in the past because of illness or injury, but I had never jacked it in before the start for no other reason than that I simply could not face it. We ended up sitting in the deserted stands at Alexandra Stadium talking and talking and talking.

'I don't know what's wrong with me, John,' I said. 'I seem so depressed and moody all the time.'

'You have been a bit of a miserable sod lately,' he agreed.

But we talked over the problem, and I think that acknowledging its existence was possibly the first step towards eventually clearing it up. And after the euphoria of that mile, at least I was more confident about the second Oslo race, the 5000 metres. Inside, I knew I could run faster than ever before. I wanted to achieve a fast enough time to warrant my selection for the European Championships in Athens (and the Commonwealth Games) without having to run in the official selection race in early August. By going back into hard training in late July and August, instead of having to earn my selection then, I could come to a better peak for the championships themselves.

So before I left for Oslo I sat down to work out the sort of schedule needed to run a really fast time at 5000 metres. My best time was 13:20.51, but I anticipated that a run of around 13:15 would be needed to ensure selection for Athens. As the UK national record had stood at 13:14.6 to Brendan Foster since 1974, that seemed as good a target as any. To achieve it would need even-paced laps of around 64 seconds each. I also estimated the pace for breaking the world record of 13:06.20 held by Kenyan Henry Rono, but at 63 seconds a lap that seemed right out

114

of my reach. So I scrubbed that, and decided just to shoot for Brendan's record.

I made sure that I attended the strawberry party the day before the race, as it certainly had not harmed my previous performance in Oslo. In fact it was only a week or so since I was last at the lakeside Panorama Sommerhotel in the Norwegian capital, and the warm sunshine was still bringing out some of the local beauties to sunbathe topless by the lake. But I resisted the temptation to go out for seven or eight extra training sessions on the morning of the race.

Instead, I jogged once round the two-mile circuit skirting the water on the soft pine-needle-strewn paths, in the company of Cliff Temple. He had just arrived from Stockholm where, the previous night, Henry Rono had run 13:08.97 in an unsuccessful attack on his own world record, with his team-mate Peter Koech clocking a surprising 13:09.50 for second place on the world all-time list. The rumour was that the Kenyans were determined to try again to break the world record in Oslo that evening. I would certainly be glad if they did try.

That afternoon Cliff and I went for a walk through the country lanes, discussing this and that, and I remarked how tired and lethargic I felt. Cliff told me his own theory that whenever the body is preparing for some major effort, it practically shuts down beforehand, saving everything for the big occasion.

'In that case,' I said, 'I only hope that mine realizes tonight's the night!'

The track at Bislett Stadium is not only a fast surface, but its location, sheltered between tall buildings in the city centre, means that there is seldom any wind to disturb the athletes. Given the enthusiasm of the local crowd, the advantageous aspects of the stadium, which looks so bleak and unpromising when empty, plus that certain magic in the air when one recalls the great names of the past who have competed and set records in the arena, there is no doubt that a Bislett meeting puts a spring in your step.

The Olympics could never be held at Bislett. It is not

big enough, with only a six-lane track instead of the internationally standard eight; for warming up the athletes have to jog round a small car park behind the main stand, meeting each other about every 200 yards. Sometimes I am happy to chat and jog with people before a race, but that night I could not stand having anyone near me. So I went outside the car park and jogged through the deserted city streets. The office blocks were closed for the night, and those who lived in the immediate vicinity were either inside the stadium or watching the meeting on television.

There were few cars and no people, and I felt totally free. However uncertain I was of my exact form, I still suspected that tonight might be something special. I felt good, and as I jogged I could hear the cheering of the crowds from inside the stadium floating on the calm, warm evening air.

Still keeping myself to myself, I went into the arena to complete my warm-up with some fast strides in my spikes. The mile was under way, and I briefly wished I was running in it; at least it would have been over more quickly. Steve Scott was once again attacking Seb Coe's world record, and getting even nearer this time as he became the second man to break 3:48. He won in 3:47.69, just 0.36 outside Seb's record. John Walker, at the age of thirty, finally broke his personal best with 3:49.08, seven years after his own world mile record of 3:49.4. For me, at twenty-nine, that was a good omen.

The 5000 metres was the last race on the programme, and up in the stands the British journalists covering the meeting were already putting the finishing touches to their stories of how Steve Ovett had set a U K record in the 2000 metres, how Wendy Sly had set a Commonwealth record in the 3000 metres behind Mary Decker's U S record. Most of them had been travelling through Scandinavia, covering a G B v. Sweden match in Karlstad and the D N–Galan invitation meeting in Stockholm before moving on to Oslo as their last stop before going home.

They admitted later that they had not expected the 5000 metres to top the earlier performances. One journalist, Vic Robbie of the *Daily Mirror*, had asked me the previous day if I was going to attack the world record, and I had told him quite openly that I was not, as it seemed out of reach.

I looked at my rivals before the start. The Kenyans, Rono and Koech, now the two quickest runners at 5000 metres, were likely to be starting fast. I would never have contemplated running two flat-out 5000-metre races on successive nights as they were doing, but the unpredictable Rono was capable of some incredible performances, and it seemed Koech was still barely scratching the surface of his potential.

The rest of the field was largely British, with Nick Rose (my room-mate on this trip), Dave Clarke, Steve Binns and Adrian Royle among the leading contenders. I needed to beat all of them, and well, to hope to achieve my aim of selection for Athens on this performance.

The gun went, and after an initial scramble the pace, to my dismay, slowed down. The Kenyans were not, after all, ready to crack on from the start. Suddenly I could see my hopes beginning to crumble before the race was half a minute old. So I moved into the lead to keep the pace going at what I thought was a steady 63-second rate. As we passed the 400 metres marker, though, the time was 61.4, and it felt very comfortable. Shocked, I slowed somewhat on the second circuit and possibly overcompensated, running a 65.8 lap to get back on schedule for Brendan's British record. But on the third lap I inadvertently speeded up again with a 61.3, still feeling good. I sensed that the rest of the field was beginning to let me go. This was not what I had anticipated at all. By nature, I am a follower rather than a leader in such races, and to find myself in front that early was somewhat unnerving.

But I was still running smoothly, with no distress. My original plan had been to take off on the fourth lap if I felt good, but here I was in front already. I also became aware that the crowd now realized that something special was about to happen. They began to get behind me, rhythmically banging the sides of the stands and chanting to keep me going. They sensed that I was either going to run a rather special time, or else drop dead in the attempt; either way, it would be entertaining . . .

After four laps (4:11.1) I was still on target for Brendan's UK record, but at the same time I felt completely in control of myself. People often talk about the euphoria of 'runner's high' or come out with the clichés about running free, but they were all true for me that night. I never once thought about the possibility of being beaten, even though I was now setting an almost irresponsible pace. It was as though my body, spirit and mind were all in harmony; I did not even think of how fast I was going. I was more conscious of the external aspects of the race, such as who was standing on the inside of the track. If I could go through 3000 metres in around 8:00 I would still be on schedule for the British record. When I passed that point in under 7:50, I was stunned. I could not work out that that meant a 13-minute pace for the full distance, but I knew it was very, very fast. My legs were beginning to get heavy but I kept the pace going.

I only had an indication of my speed when I came close to the finishing line with one lap left and saw that 12 minutes had still not gone up on the digital clock beside the track. I crossed the line at around 12:02 and I knew that I had the world record in my hand. I was able to savour that thought on the last lap, for although it was hard and I was very tired, I knew I only had to run 64 seconds to get that record, and I was running much faster than that.

In fact, the last lap was timed at 58.04, and moments before I reached the finish, the clock changed to 13 minutes, finally stopping at 13:00.41, the official time. I staggered on a few steps and collapsed on to Arne Haukvik, the promoter, who urged me to run a lap of honour. The excitement and exhilaration of what I had done swept over me and within 30 seconds I was able to start jogging again and wave to the crowd, who gave me the most marvellous reception.

An amusing sidelight, about which I only heard later, was that the American runner Ralph King, who outsprinted Nick Rose for second place some 20 seconds behind me, genuinely thought he had won the race. Apparently he assumed I was simply a 'hare' who had gone off too fast, and thought I must have dropped out somewhere. He had not seen me again after the opening laps and was unaware I was still in the race!

The next few hours went out of control, and I had no time to stop and think. There were presentations, press interviews, radio interviews, television interviews, one after the other. The meeting had ended with the 5000 metres, so many of the spectators came into the arena for a closer look at what was going on. It was bedlam, with calls from every direction.

'Look this way, Dave ... smile ... wave ...'

'Could you please spare a minute for Swedish radio?'

'First three on the rostrum, please!'

'Dave, how would you like to run in Italy next week? You would be well looked after ...'

I managed to get away from the throng long enough to ring Linda from a telephone in the British press seats. She was watching the race at that moment on television, as it had been recorded for later transmission, but she already knew the outcome as Brendan Foster had phoned her earlier from the BBC Studios in London, where he had been watching the pictures coming in from Oslo.

Linda was thrilled, but we were not able to talk for long before I was whisked away again. Sven-Arne Hansen, the joint promoter with Arne Haukvik in Oslo, had a car waiting to take me back to the hotel. He had the grin of a Cheshire cat on his face. Promoters love world records because they send the crowd home happy, entice more people to come next time, and above all they enhance the stadium's reputation as the place to go to run fast times. He had been disappointed when the world record for the

119

mile had just missed being broken, then jubilant when the 5000 metres unexpectedly turned up trumps.

When his car pulled into the forecourt of the hotel, I saw a chance to get away by myself. I told Sven-Arne I would meet him later at the post-race reception, and instead of going inside the building to my room, I jogged off towards the nearby lake. Although it was late, the sky was barely dark, and there was a tranquillity about the calm water which allowed me to reflect peacefully on what I had done for a few moments.

I found a secluded bank, sat down and let the feeling of being a world record holder sink in. It was a breathing space I needed; there would be little time for contemplation once I returned to the hotel. Eventually, I jogged back past deserted tennis courts and the running track in the hotel grounds and went up to my room.

Most of the athletes were already at the reception, but Nick Rose had very kindly waited for me to return, and he stayed while I had a quick shower and got changed. It was a relief to find that becoming a world record holder does not mean you grow an extra leg or anything else. And you still sweat.

Nick must have been starving, like I should have been, but the elation and the excitement had completely dulled my appetite. Irritating little things held me up. I could not find any socks, and my hair would not go flat. I did not want to attend the reception as the world record holder looking like Ken Dodd.

We finally got to the reception, which was well in progress by then. As we went in, all the athletes, led by Steve Ovett, stood up and applauded. I felt a lump come into my throat. I had myself stood and applauded Seb Coe after the same meeting three years earlier, when he had broken the world mile record on a night when I had been deeply depressed with my own form.

Now, to be given a reception like that was really moving. Any applause is enjoyed by an athlete, but when it comes from one's fellow competitors, it is all the more deeply appreciated.

I did not eat much. Instead, I was approached by a stream of meeting promoters, all hoping I would run in their events. Most of them said I could name my own conditions, competitors, price, and so on, if I wanted to. But I said no to all of them. I was already committed to a number of races before the European Championships and I did not want any more. I would stick to my plans regardless. The world record was a very pleasant bonus, but it was not the focal point of the season.

The British journalists present asked if they could do an 'in-depth' interview, so we adjourned to a small side room to get away from the blaring disco. But the room soon became hot and claustrophobic and I began to feel the need for some fresh air again.

The magnetic quality of that peaceful lake still beckoned, so once more, at about midnight and this time in company with Cliff Temple, I strolled slowly round it. I was still trying to get everything into perspective. I had run 5000 metres faster than anyone else, faster than every great race I remembered seeing. But that lake, around which we had jogged at lunchtime, was still there, unmoving with scarcely a ripple across its surface since.

The ruggedness of the surrounding terrain and the rocks which had been there so many thousands of years were a reminder of just how ephemeral is a world record, or indeed a man on this earth. And yet the thought that I had run faster than any other human was almost overpowering. Cliff reflected the spirit of that moment in the *Sunday Times* a few days later:

Midnight in Oslo, Wednesday. In a hotel restaurant athletes are dancing to a deafening disco while, heavier on their feet, some of the world's top athletics promoters circulate, peering into the humid darkness trying to pick out the man who, a few hours earlier, turned in a distance running performance which will live on when the world record it constituted is long since buried. They would like to talk to him.

On the bare red brick wall outside Room 415A of the Panorama Sommerhotel a telephone rings repeatedly; New

121

York, London and LA are also hoping to speak to David Moorcroft.

But half a mile away from the music and the ringing telephone, in the semidarkness of a Norwegian summer night, a tall slim figure is restlessly walking the rough path around a silent, glass-still lake, trying to comprehend how just 13 minutes of running will have changed his life.

By the time the sun rises above these pine trees, bringing the families back to the lakeside park, the whole world would know about his run in Bislett Stadium.

'It all seems so unreal,' he says. 'All those great 5000 metre races I've seen with Viren and Yifter and Brendan. And now I've run faster.'

But it is not a thought with which he seems at ease. Partly because he believes international athletics is concerned with winning, not times, and that if he doesn't win the European and Commonwealth titles later this year then he will be dismissed as just another of those who could break records, but choked on the big ones.

Not true, of course. He won the Commonwealth Games 1500 metres in 1978, but had never even broken a British record until Wednesday. But already he was worrying about what people will say, and whether he will be able to live up to his self-imposed high standards of competitiveness.

For he has an insatiable hunger, marked by this plague of self-doubt which was already beginning to surface even then, at the time when most people would be happy to sit back for five minutes and enjoy their greatest moment.

The race he ran on Wednesday also restored a refreshing spontaneity to this particular type of meeting. A surfeit of carefully planned world record attempts, some of which needed not so much a promoter as a choreographer, had left the way open for such a performance as this, if only someone would just dare. And Moorcroft proved in Oslo that it is still possible to step out into unknown territory and reach out for the limits, without needing to keep behind a pacemaker with a key in his back.

Earlier in the day Moorcroft had been gnawed by uncertainty as to how to run the race, haunted by past tactical errors, slight but magnified in his own perfectionist mind to gigantic proportions.

He knew he was in excellent form and that night he was like a bottle of champagne waiting to pop. And at last he was virtually free of injury.

It took an operation on both calves last autumn to relieve real pain which, for six years, had one way or another prevented him turning in the kind of performance to shake the world.

But this year has been ideal. A good winter's training in New Zealand, and now a stimulating job in his home city of Coventry, where he works with local youngsters in sport and recreation projects.

Apart from being someone with genuine community concern anyway, the job gives Moorcroft the best of both worlds: the time to train, without leaving a great void in the day.

'I tried to be a full-time athlete before the Moscow Olympics, because I thought it was what you had to do. But it didn't suit me. You can only train for two hours a day anyway, and I found myself getting up later and later, drinking coffee, eating toast and watching telly all day. I'm the sort of person who needs to be doing something.'

On Wednesday he had played cards after lunch, went for a walk, then decided to sit by the lake instead, but within a couple of minutes stood up and started walking again.

'This is how an athlete prepares for a big race,' he said, recognizing the humorous side to his restlessness. 'In a moment, it will be time for me to stand on my head.'

Instead, he walked several miles more, along country paths and through woods.

Now Moorcroft's biggest challenge this week is not simply the 3000-metre race at Crystal Palace next Saturday when he may be portrayed, Hollywood style, as the understudy coming in for the injured Seb Coe.

Moorcroft had always intended to run well in the race anyway against at least five other potential winners: Ovett, Maree, Scott, Walker and Rono.

Instead, the first battle will be simply to survive the sudden burst of media attention when he needs time and space to recover, physically and emotionally, from Wednesday's race.

He has the ability to win, but so do the others, who will welcome the sudden switch of spotlight to the man they had quietly feared all along.

Moorcroft, in turn, may remember his words as he went to warm up in Oslo last week, shortly before one of the most stunning and brave pieces of front running in the history of world record breaking: 'I wish I didn't feel so bad.'

We made our way back to the hotel, now plunged in darkness, and sat in the deserted lobby, revived by a couple of bottles of orangeade from a vending machine. If ever I had imagined in the past that breaking a world record would lead to wild parties, this was it!

Mary Decker passed through the lobby and stopped to congratulate me. In turn, I congratulated her on her American 3000-metre record. As we had both been put back into action by operations to relieve our compartment syndrome leg problems, there would be at least two surgeons who would be pleased tomorrow.

Or rather today. It was not long until dawn, and I knew I would not be able to sleep tonight. But already I had to try to put the record behind me and think about the future.

10

Aftermath

I went into breakfast early the morning after breaking the world record, but the telegrams had already started arriving; among the congratulations were still more invitations to races all over the world. I went out for a ten-mile run with Nick Rose, and it felt good to be running again (even though I did manage, ironically, to turn my ankle) having gone through the race repeatedly in my mind during the sleepless night.

I telephoned England and spoke to Linda again, but John Anderson was on his way to work. Still, I knew he would be chuffed because he had long been saying that I was capable of running 13 minutes for the event, and I am not sure I had believed him.

My parents were out too, but I later heard how my father had been timekeeping at a small meeting in the Butts Stadium at Coventry when the news came over the loudspeakers that I had broken the world record. Apparently he nearly fell off the timekeepers' stand in astonishment. He was working on the Massey–Ferguson stand at the Royal Show at Stoneleigh at that time and the next day he was met by local TV cameras for an interview.

Finally, I managed to get through to Brenda at work, and told her rather lamely that I would not be in that day. I felt a need to contact those people who had been an integral part of my life and to reassure them that the world record would not make any difference to me. However, the next few months were very difficult, because although I was thrilled to bits by the record, I had very little time to spend with my nearest and dearest. Instead, I always seemed to be talking to people I had never met before. It is funny how breaking a world record can turn you into an 'expert' on all manner of topics! I very much wanted to avoid a situation in which I would only be able to 'fit in' close friends and relatives in odd moments. In fact, unfortunately that is virtually what happened.

When I arrived back in England representatives of Mercia Sound, the local radio station in Coventry, met me with a car to take me home, where there was a veritable reception committee of people waiting with champagne. I was dying for some good old fish and chips, so I ended up washing down fifty pence worth of cod and chips with champagne: an unusual combination, but one which went down well this time: not like our wedding!

The next couple of weeks were bedlam. The telephone never stopped ringing, but we were reluctant to change our number, as many people had advised as soon as I broke the record. We felt that friends who we wanted to reach us would not be able to, while the people we were less keen about would discover the new number anyway.

I already had a few commitments and races planned, and I was determined not to let anyone down. The promoters of the meetings in which I had previously agreed to run were obviously anxious that I would still show up, but I reassured them. Nevertheless, it was difficult honouring those commitments while not taking on new ones. As it was, there was a stream of interviews to do, which took time and energy. But I had to stop clapping myself on the back and remember that only ten days after the world record I had to race a very important 3000 metres at Crystal Palace.

That race itself already had quite a history. Originally it was to have been the first of three 'showdown' races planned for 1982 between Steve Ovett and Sebastian Coe. After their epic 1981 season of world record swopping, in which they never actually met, and their one gold medal each at the Moscow Olympics, there was a lot of pressure on them to race each other. They finally agreed to do so on three specific occasions, starting with the 3000 metres at Crystal Palace on 17 July, then continuing with an 800 metres in Nice in August and finally a mile in Eugene, Oregon, in September.

Ovett's training had already been interrupted when he ran into some church railings in Hove the previous December, which resulted in his needing a leg operation. But his U K 2000-metre record in Oslo had shown he was getting back to top form. Coe, meanwhile, had suffered a stress fracture of the shin and had to withdraw from the 3000 metres.

The field, nevertheless, was a strong one. Apart from Ovett, Sydney Maree, Steve Scott and John Walker, Peter Koech, Wilson Waigwa and Thomas Wessinghage were among those taking part: names from my past come back to haunt me! And the man they would all be gunning for was the new 5000-metre world record holder.

The stadium was full to its 17,000 capacity and the race was held late in the evening under floodlights. There was a tremendous atmosphere. The event itself started fairly slowly, with an opening lap of 62 seconds, but I was unconcerned about the clock on this occasion. I have always maintained that actual competition is more important than record breaking, and I was getting an early chance to test my best form in a highly competitive situation.

We were led by pacemaker Mike Downes through 1500 metres in 3:48.5. Then I decided that I did not want to risk everything coming down to the last lap sprint. I had already lost recently to Scott and Maree in a fast mile, so it was important that I made them hurt from farther out. I moved ahead before 1600 metres and picked up the pace to begin what I hoped would be a long run for home. Koech, Mike Boit, Maree, Scott and Walker were all breathing down my neck, and only by sustaining a hard pace would I have a chance of loosening their grip. On the fifth and sixth laps I gradually sensed that the bunch behind me was thinning, but by the bell I still had Maree on my shoulder, ominously poised.

127

Going into the back straight he tried to pass me, and I briefly held him off. But he came again, and this time I decided that I would let him go and then try again. The crowd had been making an enormous noise, but it died slightly when Maree went past me with 200 metres left after I had been leading for so long. But it picked up as the home supporters began to realize that perhaps I was not quite finished, and coming off the final bend I kicked again.

This time Maree had no response, and I was able to win in 7:32.79, which actually missed Henry Rono's world record by less than a second and was the second fastest time ever recorded. But fast times were not the main aim, even though I had set a European and UK record in the process, breaking another of Brendan's long-standing marks.

It was a victory of which I was particularly proud, because it proved to me that I could still *race*, even from the front. Ovett finished tenth, and it was the first time I had defeated him for six years.

A week later I turned out in the AAA Championships at 800 metres, purely for speed work, and I certainly found it. I improved my personal best to 1:48.29 in winning my heat, but in the final the young Yorkshireman Peter Elliott tore away at the gun and dragged the field through a first lap of 51.4. I was already 10 metres behind everybody else at the initial break from lanes after 130 metres, and I was sprinting flat out! Fortunately, at least some of the other runners came back to me as I continued my eyeballs-out dash. Elliott won in 1:45.61, and I managed to grab fifth place in another personal best of 1:46.64. Although it was not a medal-winning class performance for a major games, it was still an encouraging time for a 5000-metre specialist, I felt.

Shortly afterwards I went to Hengelo in Holland for a 1500 metres where a pacemaker took me through two laps and I led at 1200 metres in 2:50, my fastest ever such split. I won in a personal best of 3:33.79. In four weeks, I had run lifetime bests at 800 metres, 1500 metres, one mile,

3000 metres and 5000 metres. And then the troubles began.

In retrospect, I had already done too much: too many races, too much travelling, too many interviews and other commitments. The extra calls upon my time, even if I only kept saying 'Sorry, no', were beginning to have a draining effect. The phone rang from early every morning to late every night. I really appreciated the good wishes everyone passed on, but however much I tried to keep my commitments down, they always seemed to increase. I was very conscious of not wanting to appear to have gone 'big time' after the world record, and not be available to those who wanted to speak to me. But I know now that, in the same situation, I would take that risk.

John noted how rushed the training sessions always seemed to be at that point. I was still running well, but it was with a much harder, more urgent effort than before. Training had come easily before the record. Now, perhaps because I still had to do a dozen things when I got home, I was always tense, tired and straining for the same times. I still thought I could handle everything, but I could not.

What did not help at that time was the dictatorial stance of the British Amateur Athletic Board which expected all the athletes due to compete in Athens to turn out in their one-day invitation meeting, the Heinz Games, at Crystal Palace on 31 August, or else. The BAAB were trying to bolster their own image with a new sponsor as much as anything because I think that they were finding it embarrassingly difficult to control the leading athletes. So they adopted a tough line on this occasion to impress the sponsors. Certainly I originally had no intention of competing in the Heinz Games, and the 'run or be dropped from the Athens team' approach made my hackles rise. Finally, I discussed the matter with John and we decided that my non-appearance would create even more hassle than running in a race I really did not want or need, so I reluctantly agreed to run and made a mental note of the situation for the future.

By now I was getting physically run down, with a

painful eye infection and swollen glands. Initially I did not want to take antibiotics because they adversely affected my running, but in the end I had no choice because I was not getting better. It was a depressing time. I was committed to a two-mile race against Kenyan Peter Koech at the Talbot Games at Crystal Palace on 20 August. I did not feel at all well before the race, which was being hailed as a 'world record attempt', but in the event I was pleased to be able to win in a personal best of 8:16.75, although it was 3 seconds outside Steve Ovett's world best. Koech chased me all the way to the line, though, and it was a particularly draining effort to win – nothing like as smooth or flowing as before. And when you notice that happen, your confidence starts to become eroded.

Having agreed to run in the Emsley Carr Mile at the Heinz Games, just to keep the BAAB happy, I won in 3:57.84. It was an unmemorable race. Perhaps one gets more cynical as one gets older, or, as I prefer to think, more selective. At nineteen I had been thrilled to be invited to the Emsley Carr Mile in Edinburgh, even though I almost opted for the college play instead. I was also thrilled to win the Emsley Carr Mile in 1976. But, on the eve of the European Championships, I was less than thrilled to be running in it with a virtual gun to my head. The BAAB action left a bad taste in the mouth for all the international athletes who competed under similar threats.

However, I am not making that situation an excuse for what followed in Athens. The preparatory damage had already been done the moment I inadvertently broke that 5000-metre world record, or at least when I failed to adapt my plans accordingly afterwards. When I went to Athens, my confidence was certainly a good deal lower than it had been in July. But I still felt I could handle the 5000 metres' field there, even after the heats, which seemed harder than usual.

The main threat in the final seemed likely to come from the East Germans, Werner Schildhauer and Hansjörg Kunze, and the West German, Thomas Wessinghage. I had beaten both Kunze and Wessinghage in the

European Cup 5000-metre final a year earlier, and I felt I could do so again. Even though Wessinghage had recently set a European 2000-metre record, he had been out-sprinted by the two East Germans over 5000 metres in Zürich in mid-August.

A fierce rainstorm lashed the magnificent new stadium just before the final, and some of the athletes had to warm up through dressing room corridors – not the best preparation for a major race. In the event itself I panicked. I thought I should be leading because I had already enjoyed some success with that tactic earlier in the season, but when I did get ahead of the field, I did not feel comfortable, so I drifted back and let others, including team-mate Mike McLeod and the tall Finn Martti Vainio, make the running.

The pace was slow, as everyone watched everyone else. With 800 metres left I was back in the lead again, but on that lap, the penultimate, my concentration seemed to wander and as we approached the bell a sudden rush from behind took me by surprise. With 450 metres left, I was suddenly pushed back to seventh place and badly boxed at a vital moment. It took me another 200 metres to sort myself out, by which time I think I was in ninth place, but I moved wider and clawed back some more positions. Then Wessinghage made his own bid for victory and sped off just as I managed to get up to second place.

All round that last bend I remember thinking over and over: I'm not going to win, I'm not going to win. Wessinghage was too far ahead and going well. I felt really rough in the home straight and was surprised that in the event only Schildhauer came past me before the line, to relegate me to the bronze medal. I felt terrible, both physically and emotionally, that I had been caught napping in these closing stages. But I had to come to terms with defeat very, very quickly. Having seen Seb Coe unexpectedly beaten by the little-known West German Hans-Peter Ferner in the 800 metres earlier in the week, I knew how disappointed he was; now I was the one who had to say the right things to the right people.

131

I went through with the BBC and ITV television interviews, the medallists' press conference and the radio interviews, and explained again and again what I felt had happened. I think it is important to do so, even if you are terribly disappointed inside, because we all know when we line up for a race that most of us are going to be losers and there will only be one winner. It does you good to go through the whole procedure with your head held up, whatever your inner feelings. After all, for most people any disappointment over my defeat would only last until the next event. Only for myself, and for those closest to me, would it last any longer. Everyone else was quickly looking ahead.

At least in 1982 I was able to do that as well. The Commonwealth Games in Brisbane in October would give me a chance to redeem myself. Usually, once the big games have gone (as after Moscow in 1980), that is it for the year.

There was also the Coke meeting at Crystal Palace, and a major invitation meeting at Eugene, Oregon, in between Athens and Brisbane. But it was fairly clear that I should not run, because I needed all the extra time to recover.

I had been appointed captain of the England team for Brisbane, and was pleased that Linda, Paul and my parents were all coming out to support me. I welcomed their company, although Brisbane is an enjoyable place, and the Games create a fine atmosphere. I got into my training quite quickly after the arduous flight from London, and felt far more relaxed than I had been in Athens.

A bonus came when the heats of the 5000 metres were cancelled; the event was to be held as a straight sixteen-man final. The less running there was to do, the better, as far as I was concerned. As the race approached I felt far less tense. The likely dangers were Peter Koech, the Kenyan who had pushed me so hard in the Talbot two miles and had run the 13:09 5000 metres only three months earlier, and Zacharia Barie of Tanzania, who had already been a close-up silver medallist in the 10,000

132

metres. In that race Koech had been a disastrous fifteenth, but as he had arrived only hours before the event it was hardly surprising. He was obviously a brilliant runner, but perhaps a little tired from a great many races in Europe during the summer.

I could not overlook my own English team-mates Tim Hutchings and Nick Rose either, but I felt that if I could control the race from behind early on, then make a sustained effort over the final kilometre, I could win. That is basically what happened, after Barie and Koech led in the early stages. I picked up the pace from 4000 metres, with a 64.8 lap followed by a 60.5, then sprinted the last 200 metres in 25.7 to win in 13:33.

Ironically, it was $2\frac{1}{2}$ seconds slower than I ran in Athens, but it felt far, far easier and, more important, it brought me the gold medal and some consolation. Nick Rose got the better of Koech for the silver, Nick's first medal in a major games. So three months after we had shared a room in Oslo on the night which affected my whole season, Nick and I at last ended up on the top two steps of the rostrum in Brisbane.

Afterwards, I had the honour of being one of two representatives from the England team to go on board the Royal Yacht *Britannia* to meet Her Majesty the Queen. Fortunately, I was not seasick.

My competitive season was still not over, even in mid-October. Most of the England team had agreed to go on a short tour of Australia after the Games to compete in several meetings, but these turned out to be something of a disappointment, and the Australians were quite embarrassed that they could not get many of their own leading athletes out to compete against us.

In Melbourne I took the opportunity of running another 5000 metres specifically to obtain the qualifying standard for the inaugural World Championships in Helsinki the following August. The qualifying period had come into force after my world record, and I had not bettered the necessary time of 13:26 in either Athens or Brisbane. But in Melbourne, winning by half a lap, I clocked 13:23.6, an Australian all-comers' record. This would, I hoped, allow me to proceed with the plan that John and I had concocted after the Brisbane race: to run no 5000-metre races at all in 1983 until the World Championships. (As it transpired, I went one better than that!)

Then I won two separate mile races in under 4 minutes, sharing first place with Graham Williamson at 3:56.9 in Wadonga, Northern Victoria, then winning in Sydney next day in 3:59.76. It had been a very long season, but on the way back from Australia we stopped off for a few days in Singapore, where a meeting had been planned, but then cancelled. So we had a short holiday there before completing the journey to England, home, and a long, long rest. Unfortunately, the rest was destined to be longer than I intended.

11

Reluctant Spectator

It was during the flight out to New Zealand, just before Christmas 1982, that I first felt ill. I could not eat and slept for most of the journey. On Boxing Day I ran five miles and felt really weak; the next day I was almost crawling.

On 28 December at St Paul's I attempted an interval session of 4 × 600 metres on grass, but whereas I had been averaging 88 seconds in England shortly after resuming training in November, this time I could manage only 101, 97, 94 and 91 seconds. There was clearly something wrong, and when I tried the same session two days later I had to give up, feeling really rough. I tried to keep training regardless, because part of my arrangement with the organizers of the New Zealand track series was that Linda and Paul came with me, so I felt a deep obligation to perform well in the meetings.

It was hopeless. I ran in a 3000 metres on a wet, miserable night in Dunedin, and finished almost last in 8:40. Only six months earlier I had found it far easier to run a near world record 7:32. I ran in Christchurch at 800 metres and went ahead for the first lap to try to show fight, but I died a death on the second lap and finished way back in 1:58. Six months earlier I had run 1:46. I knew I was ill because even jogging would send my pulse rocketing up.

The organizers were very understanding. They said that there was really no point in my trying to run if I was ill. So I went back to Hamilton for a while, then drove up to Auckland for the last meeting to do some television work, making on-air comments throughout the events.

The whole time I felt like death warmed up, and as soon as the programme was over I went straight to bed. I could not keep any food down, and when I eventually got back to Hamilton my illness was diagnosed as a stomach bug. I took some tablets for it and within three days began to feel better.

During that time I was due to give a talk at a local Lions Club dinner. Friends advised me to cancel it, but as quite a few people had paid for tickets I decided to go through with it. Linda attended the dinner beforehand while I stayed at home resting, then I turned up later to give my talk. I was about halfway through when I suddenly felt I was going to be sick. I said, 'Excuse me,' and rushed out. Linda bravely stood up and held the fort, explaining that I had not been very well recently, while through the paper-thin walls came the unmistakable sounds of me violently throwing up. I can see the humorous side now, but it was not very funny at the time, especially when I tried to stroll nonchalantly back in pretending that nothing had happened. It was not too wonderful an evening.

Gradually I began to improve. On my way back from New Zealand in February I flew to Los Angeles, where I had been invited to attend the *Los Angeles Times* indoor meeting and do some work for ITV and Channel 4 with Adrian Metcalfe. By the next American indoor meeting, in Dallas, I was jogging again.

I returned to England and continued training gently. I still did not feel quite right, but thought it was just taking some time to get back into a routine again. Then one day I went out to lunch with John Camkin, the former sports writer who now has a public relations and sports promotions company in Leamington, and had a glass of red wine with the meal. That night I was really ill.

At a time when I had been hoping to be back in full training again, having wasted the benefits of the New Zealand trip so far as running was concerned, it seemed there would be another hold-up. I went to my doctor, who suspected that the ailment might involve the liver, and he arranged for me to be seen by Professor Sheila Sherlock, one of the world's experts on liver complaints, at the Royal Free Hospital in Hampstead.

It was mid-February 1983, and I was about to start work on this book. In fact, I was on my way down to stay with Cliff Temple in East Kent when I went to see Professor Sherlock in London. She took some blood tests, and asked if I could come back to the hospital later that day. So I waited around in London, hauling with me a heavy bag full of training diaries; when I went back I was half expecting them to say that my blood was okay but that I had now sustained a hernia from carrying the bag.

Instead, it was more serious. They wanted me to stay in the hospital for several days to undergo a liver biopsy. This involves having a local anaesthetic, then a big needle is used to extract a small portion of liver for detailed examination. That is bad enough, but then you have to lie still for twenty-four hours afterwards to make sure the body recovers from the trauma. Lying still for twenty-four hours was probably more difficult for me than anything. I was allowed out after a total of forty-eight hours in hospital and was feeling fairly sorry for myself when Cliff picked me up at the hospital to drive me back to Coventry.

On the journey I idly picked up that day's newspapers from the car seat and was stunned to read that a fellow international athlete, shot-putter Simon Rodhouse, had been killed the previous day in a car crash on his way home after representing Britain in an indoor international match at Cosford. Only a few months earlier we had been competing together in the Commonwealth Games in Brisbane, and to say I was shocked was an understatement. Simon had always been one of the genuinely nice people in athletics and never had a bad word to say about anyone, nor anyone about him. His death was a great leveller for me. There I was, feeling irritated that I was losing some more training time through illness, while a fellow athlete and friend had lost his life. It reminded me once more how easy it is for an athlete to become so

137

overinvolved with himself that he loses perspective. Simon's death helped me regain it, but it was a bitter blow to the sport.

Several weeks later the results of the liver tests came through. They confirmed that I had been suffering from hepatitis, but that I was now over the worst of it. A rest and change of diet were needed. I had already cut out alcohol since it clearly was not suiting me, and I also eliminated cream and other dairy products, chocolate, and sugar from tea. In fact, I eat far better now and am generally more diet conscious.

The reduction of exercise meant that I put on a fair bit of weight. I even found it difficult to run steadily when I began training again, and on the track I was getting hammered by youngsters. Although nearly everyone had advised me to give up any idea of trying to get fit in time for the inaugural I A A F World Championships to be held in Helsinki in August 1983, just six months away, after missing so much winter training, I still felt there was a slight chance I could make it.

Then I started getting pains in my foot which physiotherapy could not eliminate, and also knee trouble. After several weeks I could not run at all because of the pain. An X-ray showed nothing, but later a bone scan revealed a stress fracture, a type of fracture often found among runners who try to increase their volume of training too quickly after a period off; and that was exactly what I had done.

So that was it as far as the World Championships were concerned. Although I had obtained the 5000-metre qualifying standard in Australia the previous October, now there was simply not enough time to recover from the fracture and then get in the training necessary to be in top shape by August. Instead, I had to think long term about the Los Angeles Olympics, and keep as fit as possible without running. Rest from running is the only cure for a stress fracture, and there is nothing so frustrating as not being able to run because of injury. At least while I was ill, I did not feel particularly like running. But if you are

138

basically healthy, there is a lot of energy going spare which you normally use up through running.

To keep fit and to keep my weight down, I took to pedalling a static exercise bike. A friend who owned the nearby Woodlands Health Centre gave me a key to use the facilities whenever I wanted, and so twice a day I would work on the bike for half an hour. It helped keep me in trim, and I certainly sweated a lot, but it was rather boring. Eventually, I had a bike at home which I used while watching television and video films.

That summer I began working for the BBC, making comments on international athletics meetings from the studio in London, where I was teamed with presenters Desmond Lynam and David Icke. Several early-season meetings, in Oslo and Zürich, served as test runs for the World Championship transmissions themselves, during which time I spent nine days in London, living in a hotel, and was available for studio comment throughout the many hours of athletics shown from Helsinki.

Athletics is a very popular television sport, and Steve Ovett had done commenting the year before while he was injured and unable to run in Athens or Brisbane. He talked about me then; I would be talking about him now, as he was fit and I was injured.

Once I had resigned myself to watching the Helsinki events rather than participating in them, I enjoyed myself far more than I expected. The experience of working with the BBC showed me a whole new world, just seeing the size of the operation necessary for presenting top-class international sport to a critical public.

The team, which works all hours of the day and night to produce this sort of television, have their own sort of endurance, working from 6 a.m. to 11 p.m., surviving on a few hours' sleep, then getting up to start another long day. Having seen athletics on television in other countries, I would say that in Britain we do not always appreciate the high professionalism prevalent both in ITV and in the BBC. Mistakes are very rare. To get the pictures, words, statistics and reruns coordinated takes an immense

139

amount of planning and effort. After my experience I will never watch television (or perform in a televised athletics meeting) and be hyper-critical again.

At least no British producer equalled the unfortunate gaffe of the Finnish TV director at the World Championships who actually managed to miss showing live in Finland the winning throw of their only gold medallist, Tiina Lillak, in the women's javelin. That single throw, winning the gold medal on which so many Finnish hopes were set, was probably the single most dramatic moment of the whole championships, certainly for the Finns. Apparently the letters and phone calls of complaint continued pouring in for weeks afterwards.

Mind you, I do not pretend I was perfect either. My main concern was that I did not make too much of a fool of myself, and one worry was whether to attempt to say 'Jarmila Kratochvilova', the name of the Czechoslovakian girl who won gold medals in the 400 and 800 metres, or simply refer to 'her', 'she' and 'the Czech'. Eventually I decided to go for broke and use her name. Naturally, I made a complete mess of it but managed to turn it into a joke. That was a tip I had been given by Desmond Lynam, who said, 'If you make a mistake, laugh about it. Don't try to cover it up, because it looks much worse.' Now, of course, I can say 'Kratochvilova' backwards. I only wish I could say it forwards.

I remember an occasion just after the World Championships, when I was performing a similar function at the European Cup Final meeting at Crystal Palace, when my technical equipment failed. I was sitting in the London studio watching an interview with Thomas Wessinghage, who had beaten me for the European title in Athens the year before and had just won the 5000 metres at the European Cup to make up a little for his disappointing sixth place in Helsinki. He had been talking about the difficulties for 1500-metre runners moving up to 5000 metres, as both he and I had done. Although I could not hear him properly I was suddenly aware that he had said 'Dave' and was looking at the camera. In my earpiece

I then heard the editor, Mike Murphy, say, 'Go on, answer him. He's asked you a question.' But I did not know what it was, and suddenly I was live on the air. Instead of simply admitting I could not hear the question and asking him to repeat it, I made the mistake of guessing what he had said. I replied, 'Yes, Thomas, I agree with you that running three races in three days is hard for 1500-metre runners moving up to 5000 metres.' When I saw the replay of the exchange later I found out that he had wished me all the best with my injuries, and of course my response came over as pure twaddle.

Fortunately, I had a better experience after the Helsinki 5000 metres, when Mike Murphy asked me during the final itself whether, if Eamonn Coghlan won as expected, I would like to interview him from London afterwards. Simply commenting on and responding to someone else's promptings, which was all that I had done, is much easier than having to initiate the questions, so I jotted down some notes during the race and afterwards managed to have a good conversation with Eamonn via the wonders of television.

'Hello, Dave. It's a pity you weren't here today, but I don't think you'd have beaten me!' he grinned into the camera.

When would his preparations for Los Angeles begin, I asked him.

'They've already begun, Dave,' he smiled. 'And may I say I wish you all the very best in the world for your comeback. All you've got to do is be positive. You're the world record holder, and you're the man to beat next year.'

I told him I appreciated his remarks and that I would take his own comeback from an operation as inspiration for myself.

It was the first time I had watched a whole games properly. Previously, I had usually been too concerned with my own race, but through the Helsinki World Championships I was able to follow the heats and qualifying rounds all the way through to the finals, and

141

although I am not normally very good at watching other events, I really enjoyed it.

If my own running progress had paused during 1983, several other aspects had helped to make it a memorable year. For one thing, I was appointed head of the Peugeot–Talbot Athletics Foundation. This came about when John Camkin suggested to the Coventry-based Peugeot–Talbot firm that they might be able to use me for promotions, but we agreed that to have me simply standing in front of a car and grinning was not a good idea. Instead, we set up a foundation through which fifteen young British athletes were awarded grants to the tune of £1000 each for training expenses to help them develop their potential. A panel consisting of Brendan Foster (in his role now as managing director of Nike International UK), UK women's 800-metre record holder Christina Boxer, athletics official Andy Norman and Peugeot–Talbot director of marketing Todd Evans, plus myself, was set up to choose the athletes and administer the fund, which has now helped at least some of the most promising British youngsters on their way.

Then, in June, I was awarded the MBE in the Queen's Birthday Honours List, and it was a moment of great pride when Linda and my mother travelled with me to Buckingham Palace in November 1983 for the investiture.

By that time I was also in hard training again. I had begun to get fit during the World Championships, when part of my daily routine between TV commitments was to run five miles twice a day in Hyde Park. That helped to provide basic fitness, and I agreed to run a 3000-metre track race in Jarrow in mid-September at the opening of the all-weather track in the town where local athlete Steve Cram had created such an interest in the sport by winning the World Championships 1500-metre title in Helsinki. He was already European and Commonwealth champion too, and only twenty-two.

It was a very rough, windy day, but I won the race from Mike McLeod in 8:10.22, and that helped to get me back into the swing again. It did me good to have that race before I started my proper 1984 Olympic build-up. Then, in late September, we went over to Los Angeles, where I ran a 10-kilometre road race. I finished seventh in what turned out to be a slightly short course in 28:15.

A number of British athletes had already been picked for the Olympic team to save them from having to worry about selection. But the athletes were chosen on the basis of their 1983 results, so I did not expect to be among them. Instead, I simply carried on with building up a good winter base from which to launch my 1984 track season. In a cross-country race at Ipswich which I almost did not run because of flu just before Christmas, I finished second to national champion Tim Hutchings, and felt satisfied in the circumstances. Then it was off to New Zealand again with a sense of purpose.

Unfortunately, history almost repeated itself, as I still felt ill on arrival there, this time with a sinus infection. Eventually, and reluctantly, I had to take antibiotics, which always affect my running adversely, and the combination of that and trying to diet away the extra half stone I had accumulated over Christmas had disastrous results.

My first race was a 5000 metres in Melbourne on 18 January, in which I wanted to achieve the Olympic qualifying time of 13:35. But I ran unexpectedly badly, finishing only twelfth in 14:21.3, and four days later I ran a poor 8:16 for 3000 metres. It transpired that I had a very low blood glucose level, but through improved diet I managed to recover in time to win a 10-kilometre road race in 28:57 in North Auckland on 18 February, and a week later I was able, somewhat belatedly, to collect my Olympic qualifying time with a 13:34 run in Hamilton.

Just before I left New Zealand for England again in March, I acted as a pacemaker for my friend Tony Rogers, with whom we had stayed. He wanted to achieve a New Zealand Olympic qualifying time of 3:38 for 1500 metres, and I led him through 1100 metres. He clocked a personal best of 3:36.7, and I was equally delighted with my 1000-metre split of 2:22.5. I was on the way back again!

12

Drugs, Doping and Dollars

The greatest hypocrisy in athletics is that there are two separate contraventions of the international rules which can result in a life ban from the sport for the athlete, and yet in my view they are worlds apart in seriousness.

If you either receive cash outside the guidelines recently laid down by the I A A F for legitimate appearance money, or are found guilty of taking drugs through a positive dope test, you can be declared ineligible for competition. That such differing offences carry the same penalty is utterly ridiculous. While I could never justify or condone anyone taking drugs to improve his or her natural performance, I find receiving money for athletic performance morally acceptable, in line with professional soccer players, musicians and others with skills which people will pay to appreciate.

The trouble is that the restrictions on what athletes can be paid produce an unacceptable double standard. Although I can say with a clear conscience that I have never, and would never, take drugs to improve my performance, I would have to think very hard about saying that I had never received money under the table for competing in certain athletics meetings. But if the public do not believe you on one issue, why should they believe you on the other?

Yet much of the time what athletes refer to as 'being paid' amounts to receiving a few pounds over the top for genuine travel expenses. Only a few athletes, at certain

144

meetings, are actually worth large amounts to the promoters.

Recently, the rules on payment were changed for the better, so that athletes can receive appearance money, but only at approved meetings, and with all the transactions being handled by the athlete's national federation, who hold the money in a special fund from which the athlete can then draw sums to cover legitimate training expenses. These are admittedly wide-ranging, and include such broad categories as 'transport' and 'accommodation', so presumably you could buy a Rolls-Royce and Buckingham Palace if you felt like it. The change is a move in the right direction.

Up to now a common sight at international invitation meetings has been the late-night queue outside the promoter's hotel room. Athletes from the meeting have had to wait in line to be admitted to collect their legitimate, or otherwise, expenses. For some of the lesser known athletes it might be the standard few dollars *per diem* allowance; for other, bigger, names it might be a large proportion of an air ticket between the USA and Europe, which is sometimes charged to each promoter on the 'circuit' until the total adds up to well over the cost of the original ticket.

But the humiliating aspect of it all has been the queueing, as athletes stand like beggars waiting for a few scraps. Some of the world's greatest competitors, having thrilled thousands in the stadium and millions more on television, then have had to wait for hours for their turn to be seen by the promoter. Occasionally voices have been raised inside the room as a deal is queried or challenged. The wise athlete commits precious little to paper, but that can prove as dangerous as signing a damning contract.

Rumours have abounded over how much X was supposed to be getting for a certain race. From my knowledge, many figures quoted in the press are wildly inaccurate, and even athletes themselves are often completely wrong about what their fellow competitors are getting. Or not. For sometimes at meetings where everyone has assumed the big name athlete is being paid a great deal, he might actually have agreed to compete for nothing. At other meetings, where one has assumed there would be no payments, he might have received a high figure. Only a very small circle of officials, and the athletes concerned, really know what is going on. Everyone else is guessing.

Personally I do not care who receives what money for a race, because I know that when the gun goes it does not make any difference to how well you run, if you have any pride at all. Athletes are always accused of having no pride if they turn down an invitation to run for their country. Yet it is often because they have so *much* pride that they do so. The sport is changing, and the invitation meetings are becoming much more important than the old-style international matches staged between national teams. Not just because of the money, either. Those invitation meetings are the gatherings with the best fields, the fastest times, the greatest atmosphere, and above all they are the real learning ground for the Olympics and the World Championships; far more so than a two-a-side match against Outer Slobodia. Such matches, however, still have their value for athletes on the way up. I was delighted to be picked for Britain against East Germany for my first international in 1973, but looking back I find that I have only run for Britain in international matches twice since then – and only once since 1975.

There is a clear division of priorities between officials and the most experienced athletes. They all agree that the Olympics and the World Championships are top of the competitive tree, followed by the European Champion-ships and the Commonwealth Games, as the athletes' main targets. But officials then see the next layer as being international matches, such as G B v. U S S R, G B v. East Germany or G B v. Sweden. The athletes themselves see the next layer as being the Zürich Weltklasse meeting, the Oslo meetings, the Ivo van Damme Memorial in Brussels, or the Coke meeting at Crystal Palace, for the value they give in preparing for the top layer. If you have only run in two-a-side international matches before the Olympics, where do you find experience of the pushing and shoving of a crowded international field at the first bend of a 5000 metres, where elbows and spikes are flying? How do you rehearse tactics, unless you know what it feels like to be boxed in badly while following a world record pace?

An international athlete's career has to continue upwards. There may be some whose ambition is simply to be the most capped international, or to see the world. One successful British athlete always speaks rather derisively of those team-mates who 'pack their camera first'. But I know what he means.

For young athletes, the first international is a milestone, as it was for me, and just as running for Warwickshire Schools had been. But you only get that thrill once. After that you start having niggly knee pains or slight colds when international matches come round. The B A A B is stuck with these matches because they have to provide a certain amount of competition for all events.

That is perfectly fair and understandable. The trouble comes when their sponsors and television do not want a British team composed of teenagers and fifth-string performers, or to show Britain being hammered by Luxembourg. Sponsors and television ideally want G B v. U S S R every time, preferably with G B winning, and every British champion and world record holder taking part, and preferably winning.

In the early years, of course, the athlete does what he is told. When he is first picked to run for his country he says, 'Yes, please, I'll go, thank you very much. A three-hour coach journey at the other end to a closed hotel with no food in the middle of the night? Yes, I'd love that.' The following year he will have a bad leg. The third year he will be honest and say that he just does not want to go. The public, of course, cannot understand why all these stroppy athletes do not want to run for Britain, at home or abroad.

But possibly with the advent of invitation permit meetings and appearance money, there will be more give and take among the international athletes. For a start, if athletes want to be paid as professional entertainers, and most of us do, then perhaps there should be some form of contract to protect both promoters and athletes and to guarantee appearance (subject to injury). After all, it is still hit and miss in some respects, and it works both ways. For instance, I know my name has been used in publicity for meetings, even though the promoters knew I was not coming. But the small print is carefully worded to read 'Among *invited* athletes are Dave Moorcroft, etc.' Conversely, a promoter of a major concert at the Albert Hall cannot sell tickets effectively if he can only announce: 'It will be a concert which may include Frank Sinatra. Or possibly not.'

While appearance money for athletes is to be welcomed, I also believe that straightforward prize money should be introduced into track and field events, and should greatly exceed appearance money. To the winner, the spoils. But if it does come in, an even greater vigilance will be needed to stamp out the one real menace in athletics, drug taking. For if athletes are using artificial aids, such as anabolic steroids, or indulging in blood doping, then they are destroying one of the basic principles of competition, which is that everyone starts with an equal chance.

I find it intensely disturbing, for example, that I have doubts about other athletes, in the same way they probably have doubts about me. After all, I suddenly knocked 6 seconds off a world record, and I am sure there are many people who will never believe that it could have been done without some artificial aid. Yet it was, and I hope this book helps to explain *how* it was.

The worst justification I hear for drug use is: 'I take them because others do.' Yet that is a good enough reason for some athletes, who seem too ready to cheat blatantly (even at the risk of the long term effects their totally unsupervised use may cause). When a youngster starts off as, say, a high jumper, the last thing on his mind is drugs. Yet there will eventually come a time when if he

148

reaches international level someone will suggest to him: 'If you want to become really good, you'll have to take something.' This is perhaps the single most disappointing aspect of athletics today. I can put up with the interference of politicians, because you can at least try to ignore them if you are careful. I can put up with the mistakes of officials. I can put up with the limited influence of some commercial interests. But if drug taking is as widespread as it seems, then we have a serious problem.

Although I believe in the value of drug testing at major games, all that has happened is that the cheats are more careful. The very fact that no positive tests were recorded during the World Championships in Helsinki proves how successful athletes are in avoiding being found out. As much as I would like to believe it, I do not think it shows that athletes are not using drugs in their preparation for such championships.

The only way to catch the drug users is for a widespread system of random testing during training periods, in which any athlete can be tested at any time. If he refuses, he would be considered to have failed the test. It would be complicated, expensive, time-consuming and very difficult to organize. But if that is the price which has to be paid to remove the spectre of drugs from our sport, it would be worth every penny.

The impetus must come from the I A A F. It is no good them sitting back and feeling satisfied that there were no positive tests in Helsinki. After all, everyone was expecting to be tested there. The surprise test is the most effective way. Just after the World Championships, there was a series of positive tests among weight lifters at the Pan-American Games in Caracas, followed by a sudden exodus of American athletes from the Games before they had competed when they realized they were going to be tested. Even a minimum ban of eighteen months (after which an athlete can appeal to be reinstated, and often is) would mean that they would miss the Los Angeles Olympics. Similarly, I saw at first hand the panic in New

Zealand when an I A A F drug-testing squad turned up in Christchurch at the Pan-Pacific Games and found several positive results, including one world record holder.

But gradually the surprise element at major competitions will diminish. Only when drug-taking athletes live in genuine fear that a ring at their front door could mean the arrival of an I A A F-approved drug-test squad will any progress be made.

If I feel any sympathy at all for those who take drugs, it may be over the double standards applied by bodies like the I A A F and B A A B. Over the years, to its credit, the B A A B has led the fight against drugs and championed the campaign for wider testing. But when they come to set standards for team selection for major events like the Olympic Games, they pick performances in some field events, for example, which may be practically unapproachable by anyone not taking drugs.

In middle-distance running it seems that, on the men's side anyway, the use of drugs like anabolic steroids is relatively rare. Indeed, their beneficial effects are not particularly suited to the event, although there has been some evidence that the male hormone testosterone has been used by some female distance runners with a subsequent improvement in athletic performance.

But if there is a hidden menace in middle-distance running, it must be blood doping, which is more correctly known as blood exchange, since doping as such is not involved. A quantity of blood is removed from the athlete, and then the red cells are reinjected at a later date, when the body has made up the natural loss. This is supposed to give a 'supercharged' oxygen-carrying effect of the type produced by altitude training, and although the athlete still has to be very fit to achieve success, it could make the difference between a gold medal and nothing – if it works. Some physiologists say that it does not; others claim it definitely does. Again there are a lot of unconfirmed rumours, although strictly speaking it contravenes no rules since the athlete is using nothing unnatural to his own body.

Rumours about blood exchange have particularly surrounded the Finnish runner Lasse Viren, who won the 5000- and 10000-metre titles at both the 1972 and 1976 Olympic Games. He has never admitted using the method; nor has he denied it. But a fellow Finn, Kaarlo Maaninka, a double Olympic medallist (surprisingly) in Moscow, has recently admitted that he had a blood exchange before the Games. He subsequently had a religious awakening, which apparently made him confess, but his coach at that time was quoted as saying, 'Sports have reached a point of no return. As long as you are still alive for the victory ceremony, you should get your reward. There is no room for ethics in sport any more.' If we are expected to believe such views, there seems little point in having sport anyway.

Viren's silence on the issue does not help either, although he may have been cultivating a 'mystique', an aura of brilliance, to intimidate his rivals at Olympic time. He ran at a mediocre level in between, so I really do not know how to regard him. If he did not use blood exchange in his four Olympic victories, then his achievements were absolutely magnificent, and any suggestion otherwise would be an awful slur. But if he *did* cheat in any way, then for him to have the sheer audacity to try to make us believe that he was a great athlete when he was not is absolutely disgraceful. But how do you decide?

Although Olympic success is very, very attractive and assures you a place in the history books, you still have to live with yourself afterwards. To look at yourself in the mirror every morning, knowing that what you did was achieved by cheating, would be a terrible life sentence of guilt. I can come to terms with the possibility of not winning in the Los Angeles Olympics, but I could never come to terms with winning there by cheating. Or by losing to someone who I knew had cheated.

Career Record

Annual Progression

Year	800 m	1500 m	Mile	3000 m	5000 m
1965	2:23.8*	–	–	–	–
1966	2:22.3*	–	5:09.6	–	–
1967	2:20.1*	–	4:57.5	–	–
1968	2:13.2*	4:11.0	4:43.4	–	–
1969	2:05.1	4:04.7	–	9:09.0	–
1970	1:55.8	3:55.7	4:17.9	8:30.0	–
1971	1:52.5	3:46.1	4:07.5	8:14.2	–
1972	1:53.6	3:45.7	4:03.3	–	–
1973	1:51.7	3:43.0	4:01.9	–	14:31.0
1974	–	3:44.5	4:11.5	8:07.0	14:04.8
1975	1:51.9	3:40.52	3:58.8	–	14:06.8
1976	1:51.5	3:38.91	3:57.06	7:58.6	13:58.4
1977	1:50.9	3:39.8	4:04.0	8:00.3	–
1978	1:49.15	3:35.48	3:55.3	7:43.51	–
1979	1:48.54	3:37.4	3:54.35	7:54.8	13:30.33
1980	1:48.37	3:37.5	3:55.73	7:44.4	13:29.1
1981	1:49.51	3:46.89	3:54.37	7:51.5	13:20.51
1982	1:46.64	3:33.79	3:49.34	7:32.79	13:00.41
1983 (ill)	1:58.0	–	–	8:10.22	–

* 880 yards less 0.7 seconds

Significant races

1970

28 Feb. Blackpool: 206th, National Youth Cross-Country
         Championship
1 Aug. Kirkby: 6th, AAA Junior 1500 m, 3:55.7

1971

6 Mar. Norwich: 7th, National Youth Cross-Country
         Championship
20 Mar. Cosford: 1st, AAA Junior Indoor 1500-m
         Championship, 3:55.8
1 May Sutton Coldfield: Fastest short leg in AAA National
         Road Relay
12 May Birmingham: 1st, 1500 m, 3:48.6
31 May Leicester: 2nd, 1500 m, 3:48.5
3 June Loughborough: 2nd, 1500 m, 3:46.1
12 June Edinburgh: 9th, Emsley Carr Mile, 4:07.5
24 July Crystal Palace: 6th, AAA Junior 3000-m
         Championship, 8:22.8
7 Aug. Wolverhampton: 1st, AAA Junior 1500-m
         Championship, 3:51.9
30 Aug. Crystal Palace: 2nd, Junior 3000 m, 8:14.2
25 Sep. Landau: 6th, West Germany *v.* UK *v.* Sweden
         Junior 1500 m, 3:56.8 (fell)

1972

28 Jan. Cosford: 5th, AAA Indoor 1500-m heat, 3:55.6
4 Mar. Sutton Coldfield: 12th, National Junior
         Cross-Country Championship
25 Mar. Hillingdon: 3rd, English Schools Cross-Country
         Championship
29 Apr. Sutton Coldfield: 2nd fastest short leg in AAA
         National Road Relay
5 May Crystal Palace: 5th, mile, 4:03.3
10 June Crystal Palace: 10th, Emsley Carr Mile, 4:18.5
1 July Härnosand: 4th, Sweden *v.* UK *v.* West Germany
         Junior 1500 m, 3:56.4
14 July Crystal Palace: 5th, AAA 1500-m heat, 3:45.7

1973

3 Mar. Parliament Hill: 16th, National Junior Cross-Country
         Championship

28 Apr. Derby: Fastest short leg in AAA National Road
         Relay
28 May Warley: 4th, Inter-Counties Mile, 4:07.7
16 June Edinburgh: 2nd, 1500 m, 3:43.0
30 June Leipzig: 3rd, East Germany v. UK 1500 m, 3:45.5
13 July Crystal Palace: 8th, AAA 1500-m heat, 3:49.6
17 Aug. Stoke: 1st, 5000 m, 14:31.0
14 Sep. Crystal Palace: 5th, Coke Mile, 4:01.9

1974
27 Apr. Sutton Coldfield: 6th fastest long leg in AAA
         National Road Relay
1 May Loughborough: 1st, 5000 m, 14:04.8
2 July Coventry: 1st, 3000 m, 8:07.0
12 July Crystal Palace: 4th, AAA 1500-m heat, 3:44.5
10 Aug. Crystal Palace: 7th, Emsley Carr Mile, 4:11.5

1975
12 May Birmingham: 2nd, UAU 5000 m, 14:11.8
5 June Loughborough: 1st, 1500 m, 3:43.0
12 June Belgrade: 1st, 1500 m, 3:40.7
26 July Gateshead: 4th, mile, 3:59.9
1 Aug. Crystal Palace: 1st, AAA 1500-m heat, 3:40.52
2 Aug. Crystal Palace: 10th, AAA 1500-m final, 3:51.3
30 Aug. Stretford: 1st, mile, 3:58.8
13 Sep. Edinburgh: 1st, UK v. Sweden 1500 m, 3:54.9
21 Sep. Rome: 4th, International Students' 1500 m, 3:42.6

1976
24 Jan. Cosford: 1st, AAA Indoor 1500 m, 3:45.6
13 Mar. Leicester: 2nd, National Cross-Country
         Championship
12 May Loughborough: 1st, 3000 m, 7:58.6
15 May Athens: 2nd, 1500 m, 3:40.2
12 June Crystal Palace: 2nd, Olympic 1500-m trial, 3:39.89
17 June Loughborough: 1st, 5000 m, 13:58.4
29 July Montreal: 2nd, Olympic 1500-m heat, 3:40.69
30 July Montreal: 3rd, Olympic 1500-m semifinal, 3:39.88
31 July Montreal: 7th, Olympic 1500-m final, 3:40.94
6 Aug. Edinburgh: 3rd, Coke 1000 m, 2:19.0
14 Aug. Crystal Palace: 2nd, AAA 1500 m, 3:41.63
18 Aug. Zürich: 4th, 1500 m, 3:38.91

22 Aug. Gateshead: 2nd, mile, 4:00.4
30 Aug. Crystal Palace: 1st, Emsley Carr Mile, 3:57.06

1977
22 Jan. Christchurch: 1st, 1500 m, 3:39.8
29 Jan. Auckland: 2nd, 1500 m, 3:40.3

1978
13 June Florence: 2nd, 1500 m, 3:39.46
24 June Crystal Palace: 1st, AAA 1500-m Championship,
      3:42.92
9 July Gateshead: 1st, mile, 3:56.60
11 Aug. Edmonton: 3rd, Commonwealth Games 1500-m heat,
      3:41.47
12 Aug. Edmonton: 1st, Commonwealth Games 1500-m final,
      3:35.48
19 Aug. Edinburgh: 2nd, 800 m, 1:49.15
23 Aug. Crystal Palace: 1st, 3000 m, 7:43.51
1 Sep. Prague: 2nd, European 1500-m Championship heat,
      3:40.0
3 Sep. Prague: 3rd, European 1500-m Championship final,
      3:36.70
5 Sep. Frankfurt: 1st, mile, 3:55.3
3 Sep. Fana: 1st, 1500 m, 3:36.6
15 Sep. Crystal Palace: 1st, mile, 3:55.43

1979
12 May Kingston: 2nd, mile, 3:55.1
16 May Crystal Palace: 1st, Bannister Mile, 3:56.53
10 June Gateshead: 1st, 5000 m, 13:30.33
30 June Malmö: 1st, European Cup 1500-m semifinal, 3:46.3
8 July Gateshead: 2nd, mile, 3:58.09
13 July Crystal Palace: 1st, AAA 800-m heat, 1:48.54
14 July Crystal Palace: 7th, AAA 800-m final, 1:48.60
17 July Oslo: 9th, Golden Mile, 3:54.35

1980
19 Jan. Christchurch: 3rd, 5000 m, 13:29.4
16 Feb. Auckland: 1st, 5000 m, 13:29.1
4 June Louvain: 1st, 1500 m, 3:37.5
15 June Crystal Palace: 1st, UK 1500-m Championship,
      3:41.46

21 June Edinburgh: 1st, UK 5000-m Championship, 13:41.8
27 June Crystal Palace: 1st, 2 miles, 8:18.57
28 July Moscow: 5th, Olympic 5000-m heat, 13:42.96
30 July Moscow: 9th, Olympic 5000-m semifinal, 13:58.23
8 Aug. Crystal Palace: 4th, Coke Mile, 3:55.73
11 Aug. Budapest: 2nd, 1500 m, 3:38.19
20 Aug. Nijmegen: 2nd, 800 m, 1:48.37
25 Aug. Crystal Palace: 10th, Golden Mile, 4:01.71
27 Aug. Koblenz: 6th, 1500 m, 3:39.70
31 Aug. Gateshead: 1st (equal with Nick Rose), 3000 m,
          8:01.0
5 Sep. Crystal Palace: 5th, AAA 800-m heat, 1:49.9

1981
2 Jan. San Francisco: 2nd, indoor mile, 4:01.3
4 Jan. Los Altos: 2nd, 5-mile road race, 22:07.8
21 Jan. Hamilton: 1st, mile, 3:54.37
24 Jan. Auckland: 1st, mile, 3:55.49
16 Feb. Christchurch: 1st, 5000 m, 13:36.79
7 Mar. Parliament Hill: 4th, National Cross-Country
          Championship
28 Mar. Madrid: 91st, World Cross-Country Championship
7 June Gateshead: 13th, Golden 5000 m, 13:37.51
13 June Dresden: 1st, East Germany *v.* UK, 1500 m,
          3:46.89
27 June Louvain: 1st, mile, 3:54.93
14 July Lausanne: 1st, 5000 m, 13:20.51
26 July Gateshead: 1st, mile, 3:59.53
31 July Crystal Palace: 1st, 3000 m, 7:52.57
7 Aug. Crystal Palace: 2nd, AAA 800-m heat, 1:49.51
16 Aug. Zagreb: 1st, European Cup Final 5000 m, 13:43.18
26 Aug. Koblenz: 4th, mile, 4:00.55

1982
14 Jan. Christchurch: 3rd, mile, 3:57.12
18 Jan. Sydney: 3rd, mile, 3:59.83
23 Jan. Christchurch: 1st, 5000 m, 13:36.82
30 Jan. Auckland: 1st, 5000 m, 13:31.22
6 Mar. Leeds: 4th, National Cross-Country Championship
24 Apr. Sutton Coldfield: Fastest long leg (rec.) in AAA
          National Road Relay
13 June Gateshead: 1st, 3000 m, 7:52.5

26 June Oslo: 3rd, mile, 3:49.34
7 July   Oslo: 1st, 5000 m, 13:00.41 (world record)
17 July Crystal Palace: 1st, 3000 m, 7:32.79 (European
         record)
23 July Crystal Palace: 1st, AAA 800-m heat, 1:48.29
24 July Crystal Palace: 5th, AAA 800-m final, 1:46.64
27 July Hengelo: 1st, 1500 m, 3:33.79
20 Aug. Crystal Palace: 1st, 2 miles, 8:16.75
31 Aug. Crystal Palace: 1st, Emsley Carr Mile, 3:57.84
8 Sep.   Athens: 1st, European Championships 5000-m heat,
         13:30.28
11 Sep. Athens: 3rd, European Championships 5000-m final,
         13:30.42
7 Oct.   Brisbane: 1st, Commonwealth Games 5000-m final,
         13:33.00
13 Oct. Melbourne: 1st, 5000 m, 13:23.6
16 Oct. Wadonga: 1st, mile, 3:56.9
17 Oct. Sydney: 1st, mile, 3:59.76

1983
12 Jan. Dunedin: 6th, 3000 m, 8:40
15 Jan. Christchurch: 8th, 800 m, 1:58.0
11 Sep. Jarrow: 1st, 3000 m, 8:10.22
2 Oct.   Los Angeles: 7th, 10-km road race, 28:15
17 Dec. Ipswich: 2nd, IAC cross-country race

1984
18 Jan. Melbourne: 12th, 5000 m, 14:21.3
22 Jan. Sydney: 11th, 3000 m, 8:16.0
18 Feb. Auckland: 1st, 10-km road race, 28:57
25 Feb. Hamilton: 1st, 5000 m, 13:34.0